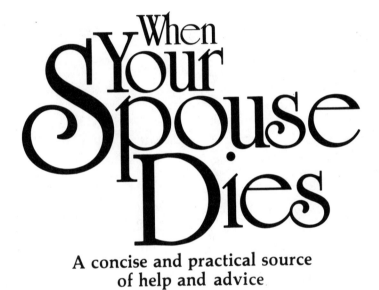

When Your Spouse Dies

A concise and practical source
of help and advice

CATHLEEN L. CURRY

AVE MARIA PRESS Notre Dame, IN 46556

International Standard Book Number: 0–87793–416–9

Library of Congress Catalog Card Number: 89–81539

Cover and text design by Thomas W. Ringenberg.

Cover photograph by Justin A. Soleta.

Printed and bound in the United States of America.

To Jim
who upheld and supported me with unconditional love
for 22 years
and gave me the strength to be a single parent

Acknowledgments

My thanks . . .

• to my children: Peggy, Dan, Tim, Julie, Kevin, Russ, Colleen, Steve and Jenny, who have challenged, encouraged, critiqued and supported me

• to the Beginning Experience Team, who taught me to love myself, the first step in learning to love God and others

• to the Dominicans, Franciscans, Benedictines, Sisters of St. Joseph of Carondolet and many parish priests who have, over a lifetime, educated me

• to Sister Clotilde Weirich, whose red pencil taught me the rudiments of writing

• to Father Guy Gau, Brother Jim Greteman, Bob Karolevitz and the Interstate Religious Writers Association, who gave me a push and said, "Go for it!"

• to Frank Cunningham and Ken Peters of Ave Maria Press, for their patience and faith in my book

• to all those who have shared their fears, hopes and tears with me, enabling me to write this book.

Contents

Prologue

It was June 20, 1971 — Father's Day. Part of me was still in room 330 at St. Joseph Mercy Hospital 20 miles away, and the other part was cooking dinner for my nine children, making necessary phone calls and thanking friends as they brought food and compassion to my home. My husband, Jim, had died of a massive heart attack the day before. I was operating out of a bad dream. How could this happen in a modern hospital with all the latest life-saving equipment? Jim was 47 years old — too young to die. Our marriage vows 22 years earlier had included "till death do us part," but death was for old people in their 80s, not for us in our 40s. Our oldest daughter had just graduated from high school. Our "tail-enders" were two and three years old. He couldn't leave me now.

In the hospital room I had gazed at the face of the man I loved, stroked his hand and asked God for strength to get through the next few days. I had to hold together. If I fell apart, wouldn't my whole family go to pieces? As a young girl I had been fascinated with a collection of rocks and crystals left by my Irish grandmother. In my mind the stability and beauty of that portion of God's creation reflected an image of God as a rock. Now I had a great need for my own rock — a stable, immovable support. Where would I find it?

The prophet Isaiah showed me the way:

> Trust in Yahweh for ever,
> for Yahweh is a rock for ever (Is 26:4).

My heartfelt prayer for trust and strength was answered. As I talked to the children, the words seemed to come from somewhere else. When their tears flowed, I reminded them of the pain, hurt and exhaustion their father had endured since his diabetes had been diagnosed 20 years earlier. We had made many trips to the hospital and the Mayo Clinic to treat complications from this disease and now his heart had given up. I told them truthfully that I could not ask God to keep him with us if it meant an invalid's life. Jim, a farmer who loved the land his ancestors had homesteaded a hundred years earlier, was not meant to be confined to a bed or hospital room. He had taken care of the necessary arrangements for his family. It was time for us to let go and allow him to find God's peace.

Gradually the children's tears subsided — except for those of one son. To this day I am sorry that I asked him to quit crying. How many mistakes I made in ignorance! At that time, however, I knew absolutely nothing about grief. Grandparents' funerals had left me unaffected, for I had been taught that when someone died they went to God. Wasn't that supposed to be a good thing?

This wasn't the same at all, and I could not deal with the feelings and emotions that were running rampant inside me. I could not handle my own pain, let alone that of the children. Burying the hurt seemed to be the logical thing to do at the time. My stoicism elicited a compliment from my doctor. He was proud that I had not gone to pieces. Controlling outward manifestations of grief made it easier for doctors, nurses and friends, but it also walled up my emotions. I could ignore and avoid the pain. As a result, my children followed the same pattern. Some of them are still dealing with suppressed grief today.

The doctor's approval reinforced my belief that it was good to show no emotion. I became a model of poise and control. I made decisions about the funeral, looked for financial advice from professionals, dealt with Social Security applications and made college plans for my oldest daughter without blinking an eye.

Deep inside was a different story. Overwhelmed, I could only see an endless, unlighted tunnel ahead of me. The myriad everyday decisions — getting three meals a day, keeping gas in the car, paying bills on time, organizing my life to include the children's activities and finding time for myself — nagged and piled up until I couldn't think straight. Panic set in more than once. Tears flowed, always at the wrong times. I was alone with no one to help me. Prayer had always been an important part of my life, but for several months after the funeral I simply couldn't pray.

Even though I could not find God in my grief, I continued to be faithful to my religious upbringing. I remained an active member of our parish, faithfully attending Mass on Sunday and occasionally on a weekday. I went through all the motions, relying on the teachings I had absorbed during my 13 years in Catholic schools. Inside, however, I was nurturing a lot of anger — at Jim, myself, the church, doctors, nurses and God. Since my spirituality was still in a childhood phase, I was afraid to express that anger. God surely would mark it down as an unforgivable sin in his big black book.

Life was full of kids, kids, and more kids. My world was closing in around me and I recognized a need to broaden my horizons with adult companionship. Continuing my college education at the University of South Dakota 14 miles away looked like a good solution. Twenty-three years had passed since I had been in a classroom and I was petrified at the thought of competing with all those young people. After years of cleaning, changing diapers, cooking meals and refereeing fights I probably had forgotten how to think seriously, let alone study.

Within a few months I gathered up my courage and enrolled in a class at the university. Passing one course encouraged me to try two the next semester. Since my self-esteem was not at an all-time high, I chose a major in Elementary Education, a familiar subject — dealing with kids. That venture kept me sane, provided me with intellectual stimulation and introduced me to a new group of friends.

Two incidents — a Cursillo and a Beginning Experience Weekend (a special retreat for the widowed, divorced and separated) — showed me that God had

16

given me abilities and gifts that I had never recognized. These not only led me to change majors and schools, but opened a new world of spirituality and brought me to a closer relationship with God. As a result of these weekend retreats, I stopped taking education courses and transferred to Briar Cliff College in Sioux City, Iowa. Thirty-four years after beginning my college career I earned a B.A. in Theology.

That degree started me in a whole new life — working for Catholic Family Services, helping with Beginning Experience Weekends and assisting with support groups for the widowed, divorced and separated. Recently I started giving workshops, seminars and retreats on prayer as well as personal spiritual direction.

Do you feel like I did, that you are walking in a long black tunnel? You are not alone. I hope to turn on a few lights as we walk together in our journey through this book. As the tunnel brightens, the road will seem shorter, wider and not as lonely, for you will see many others walking on the same path. My prayer today is that this book will be the first step in opening the door to your growth, renewal and inner peace.

It has been 19 years since Jim's death. I would like to share what I have learned of widowhood and its lessons of life and love.

One

Widowhood Is . . .

The death of a spouse is a shock to the system: physical, psychological and spiritual. It is helpful to look at its many reverberations — a multitude of feelings, emotions and actions.

Widowhood is, first of all, to *feel*, to feel . . .

- fear of the future, of being alone
- totally shattered (like Humpty-Dumpty)
- guilty . . . about anything and everything
- helpless, confused, dislocated, lost without a map
- lonely, an aching emptiness that no one can fill

- anger at my spouse for dying
  at the church for not helping
  at God for allowing the loved one to die
- envy of those who are still part of a couple
- low self-esteem
- apathetic, drowning in sorrow, withdrawn from social activities
- despair, detached from life, thoughts of suicide
- unable to pray, certain that God has disappeared.

Widowhood is also . . .

- continually wishing for "what might have been"
- hiding from oneself and others, putting on masks
- being too silent or too voluble, running around in circles
- crying . . . always at inappropriate times
- eating compulsively, having no appetite
- drinking too much alcohol, taking too many pills
- using heavy physical work to bring on sleep
- plodding through life
- experiencing stomachaches, dryness, weariness
- undergoing mental and physical exhaustion
- idealizing and beatifying the absent spouse.

Positively, widowhood is . . .

- taking a designated time to mourn
- bringing a sense of humor to the rescue
- realizing that this is an imperfect world where human beings make mistakes

20

- keeping a journal of your journey through grief
- dividing guilt into two categories: realistic and unrealistic
- taking a chance, to risk being wrong
- being conscious of misplaced and misdirected anger
- surfacing from a river of sorrow and starting to swim across the current
- calling for help on a suicide hot line
- letting go of "crutches": excessive food, alcohol, pills and drugs
- emerging from a self-imposed exile to find a new social life and new friends
- pacing yourself so work, prayer and recreation have equal time
- becoming aware of a need for help
- scheduling an appointment with a pastor, rabbi or therapist
- making decisions on your own
- finding yourself single, a unique child of God
- setting up goals for a week, month and year
- realizing that aches and pains have evolved into physical well-being
- looking in the mirror and saying, "Hey, I like me!"
- forgiving yourself for failures
- acknowledging that your spouse was not a saint, but a human being whom you loved, warts and all
- scheduling time for talking and listening to God as a necessary part of the day
- being able to list the positive aspects of being single again

21

- appreciating solitude and silence in contrast to loneliness
- filling the emptiness with love and peace
- waking up in the morning saying, "Good morning, Lord. What good things are going to happen today?"
- realizing that the shattered Humpty-Dumpty eggshell that was you a few months ago is now almost whole again
- acknowledging that your spouse is dead and you are alive
- putting yourself in God's hands each day, trusting God to show you the way.

Between these sets of feelings, emotions and actions lies what Swiss psychiatrist Elisabeth Kubler-Ross calls "grief work." A pioneer in the research on death and dying, Dr. Kubler-Ross believes that if we are to find peace and harmony after the loss of a loved one, we have to work through our grief. Where do we start? Where will we find enough energy?

Alleviating pain is a slow process. It follows no timetable. Comparing oneself with others serves no good purpose. Some people work through their grief in a year. It takes others many years to admit that grief is still a dominant emotion in their lives. Some find help in books, magazines and support groups. Others rush from one activity to another.

I have done all of those things in learning to accept Jim's death. Not until I came to the realization that I am a unique child of God, experiencing grief in my own way and following my own schedule was I able to start on that journey through grief.

What I had to realize is that I cannot run away

from the hurt. I cannot push it down inside. I cannot ignore it, hoping that if I pay no attention, it will disappear. Sliding over the top of the emotional upheaval inside will invariably cause an outburst when least expected. At some time in my life I will have to face the pain. This is what Dr. Kubler-Ross means by working through the grief.

Trying to put my pain behind brought me to many dead ends. Loneliness surrounded me. Emotional grief work drained my energy much more than scrubbing, cleaning or cooking. Sometimes I wondered if I were losing my mind. The old rules did not apply any more. I felt as if I had been dropped by parachute into a different country where I had no map and everyone spoke a foreign language.

The next chapter locates eight guideposts that helped me through the first year. Whether or not they are helpful to you, they can be a guide to creating your own. Although my life seemed to be upside down, I searched for and found many positives that helped me draw my own map and find the confidence I needed to forge ahead. You can too.

Two

First Steps

Make No Big Changes

"Don't make any big changes for at least a year."
How many times did I hear this tried and true advice?
More than I care to count. There is quite a bit of truth
behind this cliche. In the first few months after being
widowed it is almost impossible to sort out and evalu-
ate the different choices that confront us. The tempta-
tion to change surroundings, move to a different city
with a son or daughter, or go home to mother can be
very powerful.

"If I move, I won't be reminded of my spouse so
much."

"I need to get away from all the memories."

"I can't handle these children alone; mother and
dad can help."

This No. 1 guidepost, "No big changes," gave me time to make logical decisions when my emotions were not ruling my mind.

I made a commitment to stay in our small, rural community for one year. By the end of that time I would be able to sort out the positive and negative aspects of staying. The positives — a large home that was fully paid for, summer and after-school farm employment for the children, a highly supportive extended family, a well-accredited grade and high school close to two colleges and one university — far outweighed the negative list. I stayed put.

My friend Cliff, on the other hand, made dramatic changes in his life too fast, too soon. When his wife of 35 years died, he remarried within three months, gave up his apartment in a large metropolitan area and moved to a small, rural town. Stressful changes in cultural lifestyle, friends and entertainment as well as a whole new marriage relationship made him a prime candidate for illness. Within a few months he had a serious case of pneumonia.

Not everyone can keep his or her life exactly the same for a full year. Obviously there are changes in financial status which may require a move to a different home or city. The important thing is to keep changes to a minimum, acknowledge the pain and allow plenty of time for adjustment.

Be Gentle With Yourself

The second guidepost for widows and widowers is especially important if changes in lifestyle are necessary: "Be gentle with yourself." That was a difficult lesson for me to learn. My inability to treat myself with kindness was a big stumbling block after Jim died. The responsibility of caring for nine children was uppermost in my mind. I could think of nothing else. I worked at it all day every day and part of the night. There was no time left for myself. When my best friend's husband died, I was considerate and kindhearted, allowing her plenty of time to find her way back to the mainstream of life. Why couldn't I treat myself the same way?

A spiritual advisor once reminded me that "gentle" is a one-word description of God's love for me. Since God loves me with all gentleness, surely I can do no less for myself during this grieving process. I must be my own best friend.

There are many sides to this guidepost, "Be gentle with yourself." Somewhere in childhood I had absorbed the idea that all my actions should be faultless. My childhood tape keeps repeating the same thing: "Every failure is a sin." Since I never reached the angelic pinnacle of perfection, I did not measure up to my own standards.

My oldest daughter inadvertently taught me that it was O.K. to be less than perfect when she gave me a poster that read, in big, bold letters: "Supermom Lives Here." God, however, did not make me a supermom or an angel. I am a human being who sometimes succeeds and other times falls short. I grew increasingly uncomfortable with that impossible goal staring at me from the kitchen wall. Before long I moved it to the basement TV room. Eventually it disappeared altogether. I could not be both father and mother to those nine children. I could only be a good mother — and not a perfect one at that. Lowering my expectations proved to be a big step in my healing.

The guidepost of gentleness needed to be brought

out and set up many times during my journey. A few years ago I took a personality inventory and found that one of my ingrained characteristics was a preference to get things settled and finished. When I didn't get a project done in the time I had allotted, that old bugaboo, guilt, surfaced: "I'm not perfect! I haven't fulfilled my expectations." Since grief cannot be programmed, I now set short-term goals that advance me in the right direction. Those small, positive steps are incentive enough to keep me moving ahead, waylaying my feelings of guilt.

Ask for Help

There are two extreme reactions to life after losing a loved one: "I can't do anything by myself!" thinks Helpless Hannah or Paralyzed Pete. "I can do it all alone!" says Superman or Superwoman. Most of us fall somewhere in between, feeling incompetent in certain areas but confident we can handle other parts of our lives. A third guidepost, "Ask for help," continued my growth in steering away from perfectionism. When there was something I couldn't handle by myself, no matter how much I hated to say, "I don't know how," I had to ask for help from others.

Right after the funeral, my brother-in-law recommended that I take my car to a local mechanic when it needed servicing. Curly was not only a first-rate mechanic but he could understand the stereotyped woman's descriptions: "It makes a clunky noise in the front," or "It doesn't sound right." Evidently I thought that ended all my responsibility as far as the car was concerned. I was wrong.

Three weeks after Jim died I found myself and two children stalled on the interstate highway. Much to the disgust of my teen-age son, I had failed to fill up the gas tank. Because the care and maintenance of the car had not been my province during my marriage, it had never occurred to me to look at the gas gauge. I learned in a hurry. A nearby garage offered a car care course exclusively for women. We were taught how to check oil and fluid levels, the care and maintenance of tires, and the identification of different parts of the engine. At last I felt semi-competent when talking to Curly.

Other people have different problems. George was overwhelmed when his wife died and left him with four children. His nemesis was cooking. Buying groceries, organizing a time schedule for cooking after work and keeping the kitchen in reasonable order were as foreign to him as car care had been for me. When he let go of his pride and asked for help, his sister gave him a basic cookbook giving specific directions for beginners. This was the first step in gaining control over a chaotic part of his life. In the morning before going to work, he wrote down the steps for the evening meal: potatoes in oven, start hamburgers, open vegetables. This reminded him of the groceries he needed to buy on the way home. After a few weeks he was able to plan menus and buy groceries for a full week, thus eliminating last-minute trips to the store.

George found help and quick answers at the Cooperative Extension Service office in his town. Life became more orderly and peaceful as his proficiency increased.

I felt fortunate to be one of the wives of my generation who had always paid the bills and balanced the checkbook. Many of my friends left all that to their husbands and were devastated when forced to learn during this traumatic time. However, seeing the overall picture of fiscal responsibility involving life insurance, Social Security, investing money, paying taxes and setting a budget was something new. I realized immediately that this was one area where I could not "go it alone." I had to be led, a step at a time, into the world of finance.

Since Jim had set up a trust, the bank trust officer proved to be a source of great help. He took me to the Social Security office, helped find the needed papers for settling Jim's estate and recommended an account executive to advise me on the investment of the insurance money.

The Assistance Information Direction (AID) Centers and the Cooperative Extension Service in your county offer advice on record-keeping methods, realistic spending guides, savings techniques, credit management and communication skills. Universities, community colleges and high schools also offer courses to help with this immediate need.

Read and Learn

I have been a voracious reader since childhood, and that habit led me to guidepost No. 4: "Read and learn." Books were my private teachers, showing me how to work through the pain and continue growing. By reading and listening to other people's stories I was able to adapt them to my needs. I began to notice magazine articles and books about death, widowhood, grief and loss. Slowly I latched on to a few that helped me through this dark time.

C.S. Lewis' *A Grief Observed* echoed my desolation, anger and fear of the future. Here was an author who could put my anguish into words. His journey from the pits of misery, anger and self-pity to the acceptance of his beloved wife's death enabled me to start on my journey. *Widow* by Lyn Caine was a special help in opening my eyes to what grief was doing to my youngest children. *U.S. Catholic* and *St. Anthony Messenger* are monthly publications that opened up to me the fields of psychology and theology in dealing with everyday problems. The very practical *But I Never Thought He'd Die* by Miriam Baker Nye helped me take the necessary steps to solve those problems.

Keep a Journal

Reading proved to be just one step. What was I going to do with all the restlessness, anger, tears and sleeplessness? Guidepost No. 5 showed me the way: "Keep a journal." Writing my thoughts, emotions, feelings and encounters in a spiral notebook before I went to bed was therapeutic. The stress and pain of the day moved from my head to the blank sheets of paper, helping me find a more balanced, rational approach. Sleep came easier and I awoke refreshed, ready to face the new day.

Focus on Today

I still had feelings of being overwhelmed by circumstances. The road ahead looked black, and I spent a lot of time worrying about the future. Guidepost No. 6 was a poster with the motto, "Just for Today." It decorated my refrigerator door for many months, helping me to look at today's work, hurts and blessings — not the seemingly endless road ahead. The past was behind me. I could not program tomorrow. By focusing on the present day, the first stages of widowhood became bearable.

Find Kindred Spirits

My greatest need after Jim died was to find people who had the same value system, who could bounce ideas back and forth and guide me in the myriad decisions that beseiged our family. Guidepost No. 7, "Find kindred spirits," covered several "someones" — special relatives and friends whose intuitive qualities enabled them to sense my needs.

Even though my mother and father lived 1800 miles away in California, I always knew they were behind me one hundred per cent, hurting when I hurt but always encouraging and supporting my decisions. My extended family — Jim's parents, his brothers and their wives — were models of patience and helpfulness during those first months of widowhood. They listened, offered advice only when I asked and kept me from acting rashly. Small-town interest and care gave me the affirmation I needed when depression surfaced, even though it was difficult to keep up a social life where couples were the only standard.

Although I did not hear of support groups until several years after Jim died, joining one proved to be the big step I needed to get out of the "pity-pot" and start growing. The Beginning Experience Weekend, mentioned in the Prologue, introduced me to caring, listening people who shared their experiences and showed me that I too could make it alone (see Chapter 4).

Be Open to Spiritual Growth

Guidepost No. 8, "Be open to spiritual growth," grew out of the Beginning Experience Weekend. From emptiness, loneliness and tears I came to an awareness of my need for a closer relationship to God. An insatiable appetite for spiritual and pyschological reading filled that void.

I felt somewhat lost when it came to reading the Bible, for that had not been in my curriculum years ago as I went through grade and high school. Yet when I did sit down and read a passage or two from the Old or New Testaments, I could see how it applied to my life right now. The Daily Bible Study Series, a commentary on each book of the Bible by William Barclay, was the beginning of my love affair with the word of God. Books by Thomas á Kempis, Henri Nouwen, Eugene Kennedy, Paula Ripple, John Powell, S.J., and William Connolly, S.J., advanced my psychological and theological development. A bibliography at the end of this book includes some I found helpful.

1. Make No Big Changes
2. Be Gentle With Yourself
3. Ask for Help
4. Read and Learn
5. Keep a Journal
6. Focus on Today
7. Find Kindred Spirits
8. Be Open to Spiritual Growth

These are first steps that helped me on my journey. Some of them will be presented more fully later in this book. Thinking about each area, writing out my feelings, perusing magazines and books which dealt with specific aspects of grief, and finally making a decision to move ahead helped me attain my goal. Above all, I kept my No. 2 guideline handy:

Be kind to yourself.

As the months slid by, I noted my progress by rereading my journal. A mental pat on the back gave me the incentive to keep going. Slowly I learned that God loved me no matter what I did and was always there when I called. Psalm 62 reminds me to trust in God, my rock:

> In God alone be at rest, my soul;
> for my hope comes from the Most High.
> God alone is my rock, my stronghold,
> my fortress: I stand firm.
> In God is my safety and glory,
> the rock of my strength.
> Take refuge in God, all you people.
> Trust God at all times
> Pour out your hearts before Yahweh
> for God is our refuge (Ps 62:6–9).
> From *A Companion to the Breviary.*

_____ Three _____

Mourning

Tearing his clothes and putting sackcloth around his waist, Jacob mourned his son for many days (Gn 37:34).

The Jewish people, beginning with their fore-father Jacob, knew how to deal with the sorrow of death. In grieving for his son Joseph, whom he thought had died in the desert, Jacob tore his clothes, stopped all daily activity and concentrated on grief work. No, I am not recommending bizarre practices, but I do think a closer look at Jewish customs can be helpful.

Jews have specified mourning periods after the death of a loved one. *Shiva*, the first seven days, helps them through the shock and denial stages. Seated on low stools in the living room, the mourners receive calls of condolence from friends and relatives. After this comes *Sholshim*, a time when they stay away from places of entertainment, but resume daily activity and work. During this 30-day period they follow certain rituals and say certain prayers. The formal mourning is then over except for a mother or father when the grieving period extends to a full year. *Kaddish*, a liturgical refrain acknowledging the greatness of God, is repeated by the newly bereaved as a sign of their continued faith in God even after the death of a loved one. This melodious prayer, which never mentions death, sanctifies the name of God and prays for the coming of his kingdom. Herman Wouk, author of *This Is My God*, comments that "the mourner who speaks it (*Kaddish*) feels an instinctive solace and release in the act, as though for the moment he is stretching his hand to the far shore and touching the hand of his departed." Since the prayer is said in unison with other mourners at the synagogue liturgy, there is a feeling of unity with those who are experiencing the suffering that comes with death in a family.

Shiva, *Sholshim* and *Kaddish* can give us permission to go slowly, acknowledge our feelings and openly express our pain and hurt to friends and relatives. They can teach us to limit the expression of feelings to certain times and places, and help us to renew our trust in the all-powerful and all-loving God who made us.

In American society today we are slowly learning to show those feelings, although we have a long way to go before we are as comfortable as the Jewish community with the outward expression of mourning. Elisabeth Kubler-Ross has contributed greatly to this development by identifying the five stages of grief. In her book *On Death and Dying*, she labels these as denial, anger, bargaining, depression and acceptance. In caring for her dying patients she realized that these stages are typical for those who are left behind as well as for those who are approaching death. It is well, however, to note that these are only guidelines for understanding yourself or your loved ones during the bereavement period. Not every person will experience every phase nor will they have the same timetable. Kubler-Ross has opened up a new way of looking at ourselves and our actions, of identifying the progress being made and of showing that there is hope in the future.

Denial

Denial is the first stage and it hit me right away.
"No, this can't be happening!"
"He isn't really gone. He is only on a long trip."
"I am only dreaming. When I wake up in the morning he will be here."
"He will walk in the door after work tonight." This denial was necessary at first because it functioned as a buffer until I could collect myself and get over the shock. I needed time to mobilize other, less radical defenses.

As I look back on my life, I realize that there was a lot of denial even before Jim died. He was a diabetic and had been hospitalized many times previously. I did not (or could not) look at what those hospitalizations were saying to me. I ignored the long-range implications, never acknowledging that Jim was seriously ill — was, in fact, dying.

When I couldn't ignore it any more, I had a special way of coping. With nine children demanding my attention, fatigue was a constant companion. Frequently I was so tired that I was unable to get out of bed and literally slept the whole day away. It is interesting to note that I was very selective on which day I chose to retire from all my problems. It was always on Sunday. I knew that on that day the older children would be home to cope with the nitty-gritty running of the household. Letting go of my responsibilites and anxieties and just taking care of me was the medicine I needed. Like Macbeth, I found that "sleep . . . knits up the ravell'd sleave of care."

Denial is important for the bereaved. It is very necessary that our friends and relatives allow us to stay in this stage for a while. We could not deal with the loss if we did not have that time to assimilate the bad news. It is possible to continue too long with denial, but grief is a unique process taking a different amount of time for each person. Common sense tells you or your loved ones how long that should be. Calling a therapist, minister or pastoral counselor for advice is a good step to take if you have any doubts.

Anger

Anger shoots out in all directions and triggers many other emotions. Don't be surprised if you find your anger is displaced or projected on those around you. Children, parents, church, life-long friends and co-workers will get the brunt of your angry feelings. Sometimes we alienate ourselves from family and friends, and this in turn makes us more angry at ourselves. It seems like a vicious circle with no way out.

• We may be angry at God. "Why me? I have always been a good Catholic, attended Mass every

Sunday, gone to confession and communion, taught CCD, contributed to the support of my church, obeyed your commandments, followed the church's proclamations on birth control, and now, God, you do this to me! It is not fair!"

"Why did I ever have all these kids? God, this whole mess is your fault. You knew I would have to raise them alone!"

Anger churned inside me for a long time. "God, I am so angry that you did this to me!" was more than I dared to say. As a child, wasn't I taught that anger was sinful? The all-powerful God would surely lash back for expressing that forbidden emotion. Didn't the Bible say that God struck down the Philistines? "If I tell God how angry I am, something terrible will happen to me."

"Why couldn't you take somebody who is older, God? Jim is too young and we need him too much!"

"God, why are you punishing me? What have I done wrong?" The belief of Job's "comforters" — that death, sickness and tragedy were punishment for sins — seemed to be alive and well in me. Since Bible history 40 years ago was my only exposure to the scriptures, a mature understanding of God's word was a long way from being part of my faith.

• We may have anger at those who express condolences.

"I understand just how you feel!"

"You wouldn't want him to suffer."

"He is at peace now."

"Only the good die young."

"God must have wanted him in heaven."

None of the above eased my pain. Though meant to be comforting, they were the last things I needed to hear from friends. I was a bundle of feelings. What I needed was someone to acknowledge those feelings — not advice.

"God sends these trials to test us."

My mind rejected that statement. Even in my deepest grief I was sure that God was not "testing" me. I would not inflict my children with bad events to see how they would react. As my loving parent, God would not do that either.

"God never sends us more than we can handle."

This may be true, but right at the moment there was an insurmountable mountain staring me in the face. I couldn't see around it. Shock and anger alternated with hopelessness, and I needed someone to walk with me, listen to me and give me some hugs. I needed to know that somebody cared.

"I'm sorry" is the easiest and kindest thing to say.

"I know it hurts, but I will walk with you and listen when it gets too difficult to handle by yourself."

This promise to stand by me in my aloneness can be most consoling, but please don't forget that promise. Come and see me four to six weeks after the funeral when everyone else has gone and I am deserted.

• We may be angry at our spouse.

"How could Jim possibly leave me with all these children to raise by myself? That was a dirty trick!"

"Jim didn't care for himself and his diabetes the way he should have. I think he wanted to die and leave me." (Logic is not one of my strong points when I am angry.)

Anger can make us miserable if we stuff it down inside and don't acknowledge it. Rest assured that those suppressed feelings will pop up sometime in an inappropriate way. Used properly, anger can be a motivating force that helps us move ahead — if we let it.

A favorite poster that helps me handle anger more appropriately says: "Feelings are not right or wrong. They just are." The feelings themselves are not wrong. Anger is not a sin. How we use that anger in our lives can be negative (sin) or positive (life-giving). We may choose to scream, yell, retreat into coldness and silence, or lash out at those around us. We may choose to name our angry feelings, look for the cause, purify our motives, uncover any hidden anger and express the emotion in an appropriate and positive manner. The choice is ours. God has given us free will. We can turn away from him or use this occasion to grow in his love and grace. Keeping a journal of your feelings, and writing exactly how angry you are at God, your spouse, your children, yourself or anybody else who happens to be within range is a good way to defuse this anger. No one else need see your journal; it is your private therapy notebook. Putting your feelings down on paper reduces the feeling of helplessness and lack of control. Emotions quit circulating in your head when they are written down.

Re-reading my journal three to six months after Jim's death provided a yardstick for measuring my progress. I could see how I had grown and worked through some of my grief. Usually I was able to say, "Did I really feel like that? I sure don't now!"

Another way of venting anger is to talk to someone about feelings. A friend who is open and willing to listen without giving advice can be very helpful. Your pastor, doctor, priest, minister or rabbi are also good sounding boards for this kind of listening. They may advise you to seek professional counseling if they think it is necessary.

Telling God how I feel is another way I am able to reduce my anger and helplessness. John Powell, S.J., a popular author and speaker on Christian living, says that "the first thing I try to do is tell God who I am. That keeps changing. I'm different every day. I am a different person today than I was yesterday because I have prayed and laughed and cried since yesterday. So I try to tell God who I am at this very moment — how I feel" (*Praying,* July–Aug. 1987).

This was a new way of praying for me. God and I are much closer since I opened up to him. I pulled down a wall that was dividing us, and in doing so, I was open to exploring a new facet of my inner self.

Bargaining

Trying to enter into an agreement with God is known as bargaining. I entered the third stage even before Jim died.

"If you help him get better, Lord, I will go to Mass every day."

"If you will only cure him, Lord, I will be the best wife and mother there ever was." (Promises! Promises!)

Yes, bargaining does look short-sighted, and to a certain extent it is. We cannot bear to look further into the future. We are only concerned about today.

After Jim died, I found a different way to bargain: "Since I can't possibly raise these children alone, you find me another husband, Lord, and I will go to church, be the best mother and wife there is,

42

and try to talk one of my children into being a priest or sister." (I was desperate.)

I wonder if God smiled when he heard my prayer. I guess he knew I wasn't ready for another marriage. Very likely most men, realizing that nine children came along with me, were not ready for that either. Incidentally, none of my children is in the seminary or convent.

Retaining my sense of humor was a prime requisite in dealing with this stage. As an alternative to the crying, it was invaluable. When I was finally able to look at myself more objectivly, I had to laugh. God had waited for me to realize how futile and silly this bargaining was. I had many steps to take on my journey.

> They that love mirth, let them heartily drink,
> 'Tis the only receipt to make sorrow sink.
> — Ben Jonson, *Entertainments*

Depression

Anger and rage were replaced with a sense of great loss, and the next stage, depression, set in. A depressed person feels helpless, floundering, low and lifeless. Guilt and anger turned in on oneself are the basis of this stage.

Anger at myself brought a load of guilt into my life. It was a long time before I could dump that by the side of the road. "If I had watched over Jim's diet more faithfully, made sure he didn't steal any snacks or sweets and checked on his urine tests, he wouldn't have died. I am a failure because I did not take care of him properly."

Could I have honestly spied on Jim and treated him as a child, forbidding him to eat sweets? Wasn't he an adult, responsible for his own life and health? God had given him free will. This had to be unrealistic guilt.

"I neglected Jim because of all the children. There was always someone needing or demanding attention. I did not make him the top priority in my life. It is my fault he died."

Not only was I responsible for my own life and the lives of nine children, but I managed to take responsibility for his life too! Did I think I was God?

Neither Jim nor I were able to express our deepest feelings to each other. We had been brought up to bury our emotions and we did not grow out of that while raising our family. My next grieving stage was to take responsibility for our lack of ability to communicate.

"If I had been a true friend and confidante, Jim would not have experienced so much stress and could have lived longer."

Today I know more about relationships and communication, but during our marriage I did my very best. (Regret but not guilt.)

Sometimes I used if, should or ought statements.

"I *ought* to have been more careful and helped Jim with his urine tests and diet. Then he would not have died."

"*If* I had spent more time with him, and less with the children, he would not have died."

"I *should* have been the perfect wife and done more for him." Most of these guilty feelings were unrealistic. It was obvious that perfectionism had a deep hold on me. God had made me a human being, not an angel. Awareness that it was O.K. for me to be human spurred my journey through the grief process.

Keeping a journal was again my lifesaver, helping me to distinguish between the different kinds of guilt, realistic and unrealistic, and forcing me to look at my feelings, expectations, emotions and foibles in black and white. Seeing the words *if, should* and *ought* in my notebook helped me to say: "I did the very best I could at that time in my life with the tools and knowledge I had at my disposal. I know more about it now, but that does not mean I was guilty of neglect. Both God and Jim love me even though I am not perfect."

In dealing with depression a support group for the widowed, divorced and separated helped me sort out my feelings and integrate new concepts in my life. The weekly meetings, facilitated by others who had experienced loss in their lives, helped me over the rough spots and taught me to cope with those varying stages of grief: denial, anger, bargaining, depression and acceptance.

The lists of social activities in newspapers and church bulletins offer help when we are ready. Some groups are for the widowed only, some for divorced and widowed and some for all who are dealing with the loss of a loved one. There are many people who open their hearts and bring healing to themselves and others. We have only to reach out and ask for help.

If depression seems to go on too long, if there are signs of personal neglect, withdrawal or change in life habits, then we may need the help of a trained therapist or counselor. Medical doctors, the local hospital, the yellow pages of the phone book or recommendations from friends are sources of information. Call your priest, rabbi, minister or church social service office for suggestions.

If a friend or relative suggests that you see a counselor, it is wise to listen closely to that person. Immersion in grief does not permit us to step back and look at the overall picture. Someone who loves or works with us can frequently be a better judge of our needs. A therapist can help us out of our depression and find a new perspective on life.

Acceptance

Yahweh is near to the broken-hearted;
he helps those whose spirit is crushed (Ps 34:18).

Learning about these stages and becoming aware of how I was using them was helpful. Awareness taught me to reflect on my goals and to direct my actions. Slowly I saw that I was a human being who had tried. Sometimes I succeeded and sometimes I failed. I realized that I could not be perfect, and that was O.K. I moved into the final stage, acceptance.

Acceptance does not mean resignation or intellectual agreement with the status quo. Acceptance brings a peacefulness, a realization that God loves us so much he will always help us over the rough spots. It was difficult to imagine how God could love me when I had so many feelings of anger, fear, guilt and pride. Reading books which focus on spirituality finally showed me that God's love is a gift. I can do nothing to earn that love. I have only to open my heart and let it in. When I accept that love, trust and

46

faith, God's guidance becomes an integral part of my being.

Gradually I accepted Jim's death as part of God's plan. I accepted myself as a unique child of God who would make mistakes now and then but would continue to grow and walk with Christ.

The stages of grief will not come in a neat order, moving from one to another on a given timetable. Dr. Kubler-Ross offers them as tools to help us understand our behavior. In climbing the mountain of grief we do not move from one plateau to another and then slide home free after we have reached acceptance. It is more like the waves on the ocean during an angry storm. We may start with denial, move to depression, scream out in anger, bargain with God and then fall back into denial or depression. Each time we do this, however, the crest of the wave will not be quite as high, the trip down not quite as low. Gradually the storm within tapers off, leaving a relatively calm sea with only a few ripples.

It is good to pass through these stages, not jump over or bury them deep inside. Many people never move on to other things in their lives. They remain stuck in one stage or another. We can come to a full acceptance of these events if we work them through. Don't be afraid to feel the pain. Find someone who can help you. This is where support or grief groups are so valuable. There you can find others who can understand the pain and hurt you are feeling and walk with you along the way.

A friend of mine, Joyce DeMaro, wrote a prayer for a support group which put into words what I needed to say to God:

Loving and accepting Father, guide us in our attitudes and actions to examine the grief process as we work together toward a peaceful acceptance of our personal loss.

Help us to gain the courage and strength necessary to make changes for growth and understanding not only in ourselves but toward others who are suffering through their losses. Amen.

_____Four_____

Being Single and Lonely

Yahweh God said, "It is not right that the man should be alone. I shall make him a helper" (Gn 2:18).

After 22 years of marriage, I agreed with Yahweh God. It is not good for anyone, man or woman, to be alone. Who would come in at night, put his arms around me while I was fixing supper and give me a hug? Who would remind me of alternative solutions when I got so angry that I couldn't think straight? Who would say, "Let's get a baby sitter and go to Minneapolis for a football game"? Who would rub my back when we got in bed at night, helping me to relax after a day of chasing kids? What I was really asking was, "Who would take care of my needs?" God had made us to be together, and here I was all alone.

Webster's Dictionary gives a definition of "lonely" as "standing apart from others of its kind." I can think of no better description of myself during the first year after Jim died. I knew I stuck out like a sore thumb wherever I went — church, shopping mall, restaurant, even picking up my mail at the post office. There was a big "W" stamped on my forehead (at least in my own mind) and it was never going to wash off.

As I look back, I see that a nurturing, supportive network of people was helping me through the transition from being one-half of a couple to being single again. I was not alone. The blinders of grief prevented me from seeing all the help that came my way.

Jim and I had belonged to a bridge club which met for a monthly dinner and card game. Much to my joy they insisted that a 13th member was absolutely essential to the well-being of the group. Only then could the hostess clean up the dishes the night of the party, letting me substitute in the bridge game. They were my "bridge over troubled waters." Today I still play cards and join them for weekend vacations.

In other groups I felt like a fifth wheel. It took awhile before I could understand that the subtle changes and problems in my social life were partially self-induced. I didn't know how to handle myself in the world of couples. In our small-town society, the men usually gathered together and talked about business and farming. The women clustered at another table to discuss home, children and town news. As much as I wanted to be part of the women's group, I also enjoyed talking to men. Frequently it was the only chance I had to hear a masculine point of view now that Jim was gone. But if I joined the men in conversation, what would their wives think? That I was making a play for another husband? I wasn't, but how could they know?

I also recognized that both the men and women were uncomfortable in my presence. I reminded them of their own mortality.

"This could be me, if my husband died."

"Sometime I will be dead, and my wife will be here alone, just like Cathy."

Slowly I realized that I needed a social life with singles as well as couples. Venturing outside of the familiar couple-oriented society petrified me. Singles who could offer friendship with no strings attached were few and far between in our small community, and I did not know where to start looking. I felt like a teenager, but a mirror told me I was long past that stage in my life.

A course in rocks and minerals led me to become a member of a local rock club and to find a new set of friends. Another widow and I became friends through a university-sponsored tour. Acknowledging that adult conversation and ideas were needed as much as companionship, I started taking one or two courses a semester at a nearby university. This opened up new aspects of learning in areas such as psychology, history and education. My world was expanding.

Beginning Experience

A few years after Jim died I participated in a Beginning Experience Weekend. This program is designed to help widowed, divorced and separated people work through some of the pain, anger, grief and depression that follows the loss of a love. Through peer ministry, in the atmosphere of a retreat, time is provided for people to re-evaluate their lives, find the light of hope and move on to a new beginning. Although written originally by Catholics, the program has always been open to men and women of all faiths.

Beginning Experience turned my life around. This group of singles not only guided me through the grieving process during the weekend, but invited me to continue my growth and development through membership on their team. I recognized God's loving, guiding hand in my life. The concern and unconditional love from this group convinced me I had found my home. I wanted to "reach out and touch someone" as I had been touched. Not only was I able to help others who were grieving due to death, divorce or separation, but by talking to priests about this group, I was able to help the clergy understand the needs of the bereaved, thus keeping a vow I had made when Jim died.

Blue Days and Blue Skies

Certain days of the year are blue days. I am tired, depressed and want nothing more than to quit everything and go to bed. If I look at the calendar, it probably is an anniversary — engagement, wedding, Jim's death — or a holiday like Christmas, New Year's, Thanksgiving or Easter. Mental health experts know that these normally happy, family holidays are "down" times for the bereaved, causing us to feel extra lonely.

I decided to make our first Christmas without Jim a very special one and really go all out on presents. I spent more for the children's gifts than I had ever done before, and it was great to see their eyes sparkle when they opened them. The next year rolled around and it was necessary to get back to a budget Christmas. Spending the extra money did not ease the pain. It just gave me something else to worry about — paying the bills for the next six months.

A much better idea occurred to me several years later. When their father died, the children ranged in age from 18 to 2. My youngest daughter, Jenny, told me that she had absolutely no memory of her father, and that made her very angry — at him and at God. So I asked each one of the older seven children to write out at least one page of some special memories of their dad. Those letters, filed in a notebook, were given to the two youngest children for Christmas. It was healing, not only for Steve and Jenny, but the older ones also reported that they worked through a lot of grief and experienced much healing as they wrote.

With nine children, four in-laws and five grand-children, you can guess that Christmas is a wild time at my house. I usually don't have time to do much mourning or feeling sorry for myself. That is different for other families I know. It is a time of intense depression for many people. I usually save all my blue feelings for New Year's, after all the Christmas hustle and bustle are over.

Jim and I married on December 29. On our honeymoon in Chicago, we had danced to Eddy Howard to ring in the new year, 1949. In the following years we made that holiday a very special night for the two of us and I feel very depressed when I have to spend that evening at home. Since his death I have done everything imaginable on December 31. I have gone to movies, crashed parties, checked out the bar scene (bad choice) and gone to a country club dance (another bad choice). I was a single with all those couples.

My best New Year celebration was attending a prayer service and eucharistic liturgy with the Beginning Experience team. We saw the old year out and the new year in with conversation, prayer, communion, singing and breakfast — a quiet, peaceful way to celebrate. God had blessed me with special friends who helped me through the tough times.

Participating in Memorial Day ceremonies at our local cemetery used to be a yearly ritual for Jim and me. The first few years after his death I insisted on attending and always ended up in tears. Finally I realized that God did not give me a commandment written in stone: "Cathleen, attend Memorial Day ceremonies." It was all right to change routine traditions; I was not dishonoring Jim's memory. Now I visit his grave several days ahead of time, bring flowers, remember good times and pray that he and God will help me through the next year. And they do.

Over the years I have learned how to get the best of those depressed feelings by planning my anniversaries and holidays ahead of time so I don't sit at home feeling sorry for myself. By reaching out and finding someone to celebrate in a new way with me, I can change the blue days to blue skies.

Friendship

Luisa, my close friend and confidante, is a very special person in my life. If I need someone to help

me blow away the overcast skies that frequently surround me, I know I can count on her presence, understanding and help. She can put me back on the
right track, bring a smile to my lips with her sense of
humor and let me know that she loves me just the
way I am today.

Such a friendship is very important, for we need
people at many different levels of our lives. We need
friends who are interested in our work, activities,
hobbies and recreation. We need someone who
shares our value system and outlook on life. Our
deepest need, however, is for a close friend, a kindred spirit who loves us unconditionally, allows us to
be totally open and honest and shares our feelings,
experiences and thoughts.

No one human being can fill all those needs. We
have to broaden our world, reach out and find several
friends, each one of whom has special gifts that com-
plement our abilities. It is good to remember that God
sends many people into our lives. If we are open to
meeting new people and willing to form new friendships, we will find those who can talk, laugh and play
with us.

The love of my friends images God's love and
friendship. God, too, is my friend. Jesus told his dis-
ciples, "I shall no longer call you servants . . . ; I call
you friends" (Jn 15:15). The prophet Isaiah says that
God never forgets me (Is 49:15). To ensure that I understand this, God sent his Son to me. Jesus is always
here, waiting patiently for me to share my thoughts,
feelings and experiences. He is available day and
night, ready to listen and comfort me.

How do I nourish that friendship? How do I teach
myself to spend time with him, listen to his advice

and enjoy his presence? Chapter 5 goes into more detail about nurturing one's relationship with God. For now I will say that reading about prayer and hearing other people's stories has taught me that there are many ways to develop that relationship. Usually I get one or two insights from each article or book that help me develop that friendship.

Loneliness

Loneliness leaves its traces in man but these are marks of pathos, of weathering, which enhance dignity and maturity and beauty, and which open new possibilities for tenderness and love. . . . Loneliness is as much a reality of life as night and rain and thunder and it can be lived creatively. So I say let there be loneliness, for where there is loneliness, there is also sensitivity, there is awareness and recognition of promise (Clark Moustakas, *Loneliness*).

Loneliness is not labeled "For Singles Only." It is a human experience. Everyone has a story of how they have experienced loneliness. The small child, the adolescent, the single adult, married people and the elderly person in a nursing home all feel lonely sometimes. There are occasions when we feel insignificant, isolated, unimportant, not part of the group. One woman says it well: "When I'm lonely (I am) isolated not by choice, unable to make myself heard, understood, seen, accepted, valued, loved. Physically, it's an acute attack of skin hunger. I ache to be held, stroked" (quoted in an article in *St. Anthony Messenger*).

There are occasions when we feel insignificant, isolated, unimportant, not part of the group. If we look back on our married life, most of us can admit there were many times when we were lonely. Marriage does not mean we will *never* feel lonely, any more than singleness means we will always be lonely. Feelings of being abandoned and isolated do not disappear because of something or someone outside ourselves.

"Acute skin hunger," the need to be touched, loved and hugged, the need for sexual fulfillment, attacks all of us at one time or another as we adjust to our widowhood. We should not be ashamed of such feelings. God made us with these desires, and they are good. Like all emotions, however, they can be used in positive or negative ways. What will be our choice? Will we be afraid of them, withdrawing from a social life because we don't trust ourselves or others? Or will we go to the opposite extreme and jump into bed with every available partner? Most of us probably fall someplace in the middle — not withdrawing completely, but having times when we are aching for someone to hold and love us. How do we deal with this very real need?

There are several questions we need to ask ourselves: "What do I really value? What do I believe about sex and marriage? Is there any other way besides sexual intercourse to handle sexual feelings? What is right for me at this time of my life?"

My strict Catholic upbringing had influenced my value system to such an extent that at first I was terribly afraid to show any interest in the opposite sex. There was an invisible 10-foot pole between me and any man. I not only did not trust men, but I didn't trust myself either.

Growing in my own self-esteem helped me find

new friends and form new relationships. It took much reading, studies on informed conscience, and a lot of frank discussions with friends and counselors before I could say, "I cannot handle a sexual relationship outside marriage. Physical attraction is only part of the story. For me, love is a total giving of myself to the relationship — emotionally, intellectually and spiritually as well as physically." Having decided that rationally, however, did not mean I had solved the problem.

I had tried all the old recommendations. Cold showers, pacing the floor, watching late-night TV and reading a good book, which involved me in someone else's story, were effective at times. Cleaning out a closet, scrubbing the floor, sweeping out the garage, housecleaning, mowing or raking the lawn, a good brisk walk, jogging or a tennis game also can be productive outlets for sexual energy. But all this activity was not helping me with that overpowering need for sexual fulfillment and communion with another. How could I deal with that very real need for physical closeness? How did other widows handle this problem?

Lyn Caine, in her book *Widow*, says very frankly that masturbation is a temporary answer for sexual tension, but it surely is no substitute for a sex life. Her statement that masturbation "reinforced my knowledge of myself as a sexual being," set me on a new line of thinking. How well did I know myself, and how well did I know the theological and psychological principles in the area of sexuality?

I had grown up believing that masturbation was a "mortal sin" in addition to causing all sorts of physical and emotional illnesses. Deep-seated guilt finally forced me to look at the teachings and reflections of theologians, psychological experts and the church. What were they saying about this? In developing an informed conscience we need to look at all aspects and then make a decision.

A recent statement by the Catholic Church says that masturbation "lacks the sexual relationship called for by the moral order, namely, the relationship which realizes 'the full sense of mutual self-giving and human procreation in the context of true love'" (*Declaration on Certain Questions Concerning Social Ethics,* USCC). This understanding is the ideal to which we are all striving.

Some theologians hold that masturbation is a sign of emotional immaturity, needed for a time but, it is hoped, abandoned as the person matures. I could easily label myself as "emotionally immature," for I had spent a lifetime being dependent on two men: my father and my husband. Now, in my widowhood, I was learning that my wholeness did not depend on my relationship with a male.

In his book *Embodiment: An Approach to Sexuality and Christian Theology,* James B. Nelson suggests that growth in sexual development can be marked on a continuum: complete independence to complete dependence. Neither extreme is advisable. We are not self-contained lovers, nor are we radically dependent on another mortal in order to love. We need interdependence, drawing as we need from both ends of the continuum. As St. Benedict recommended, "Moderation in all things."

Psychologists look for the meaning behind the act of masturbation. Is it done for pleasure, comfort, release of tension? Is it used as a neurotic escape or withdrawal from risky, new relationships? If it is used as a retreat from moving forward, we need to ask ourselves if we have taken the wrong road.

Psychologist June Singer says, "What is most important [is] that if one is open to . . . the value of masturbation, then a sexual relationship with another person becomes a matter of choice rather than a matter of necessity" (*Androgyny: Toward a New Theory of Sexuality*). If it is used in this manner, it could be a short-term solution to an immediate need.

Long-range help from friends, family and support groups helped me mature and develop beyond that need. I learned new, more mature ways of dealing with my sexuality. My peers, the widowed and divorced, understood my emotions, greeted me with big hugs, had plenty of time to listen with complete attention and assured me that I was not the only one having those feelings. They respected my value system, offering to walk with me through this difficult part of my journey. Their hugs did much to alleviate my "skin hunger" without resorting to one-night stands or jumping into a new relationship before I was ready.

Formation of conscience is not a quick and easy process. Each one of us has to study those three areas — church teaching, theology and psychological insights — and form the best possible solution for our individual self. Bernard Häring states the goal: "Everyone, of course, must ultimately follow his conscience; this means he must do right as he sees the right with desire and effort to find and do what is right" (*The Law of Christ*, vol. 1).

How do we move from the experience of overwhelming loneliness to "the recognition of promise" that Clark Moustakas sees as the challenge in our lives? How do we move away from the sporadic or chronic feeling that everyone — including God — has deserted us? Moustakas says: "We must learn to care for our own loneliness and suffering and the loneliness and suffering of others, for within pain and isolation and loneliness one can find courage and hope and what is brave and lovely and true in life. Serving loneliness is a way to self-identity and to love, and faith in the wonder of living" (*Loneliness*).

Many years after my husband died, when the last child went off to college, I experienced a serious bout with depression due to loneliness. For the first time in my life I was alone in a house and I did not know how to cope with the emotion. For 34 years I had been raising children. Now that the children were gone, what would be my goal in life, of what use would I be to the world?

Christopher Kiesling, O.P., says that there is a need to face this feeling of isolation, own it, and see it as the negative side of longing for God. Prayer is a constructive response to loneliness. Seeing loneliness as an invitation to a deeper encounter with myself, God and others is the only way out of that pit of desolation. We can learn to be comfortable with our aloneness.

Overcoming Loneliness

In his popular book *The Art of Loving*, psychiatrist Eric Fromm claims that people trying to overcome loneliness have four tendencies. The first is to sink back into nature — to operate on instincts alone and abandon reason. Easing the pain with drugs or alcohol, refusing to make decisions, following old habits mindlessly and promiscuously rushing from one partner to another are examples of this stage. We look for a cure from outside of ourselves.

Jim and I had always enjoyed a drink before dinner after he came in from working on the farm. After he died, I saw no reason to discontinue the practice. It was a remembering time for me, a time that brought him closer in the depths of my loneliness. Soon I was waiting for 5 p.m. to roll around so I could have that drink — sometimes more than one. My oldest son came in one evening, saw a drink in my hand and berated me: "Mom, do you realize you are having a drink every night? You are going to become an alcoholic!"

Of course I denied it, but that expression of concern made me aware of what I was doing. From then on I made a consistent effort to watch the TV evening news, write a letter, visit with a neighbor — anything so I would not be in the kitchen fixing myself a drink. It wasn't easy. Many evenings I paced the floor, asking for God to help me get over this need. I now can enjoy a cocktail or glass of wine, but I am not using it as a cure for my loneliness. I am more likely to use food to submerge my feelings, a practice which is just as compulsive as drinking. Again I am asking for God's help.

According to Fromm, the second tendency of the lonely is toward conformity — to get lost in the crowd. Do exactly what everyone else is doing in order to be part of the group. Don't question your motives or anyone else's. Don't do anything to stand out in the crowd. Develop a grey, unobtrusive personality. Don't try anything risky, anything that will call attention to yourself. Some widowed people withdraw from all social activity, spending all leisure time in front of the TV set. The Bible's statement that it is not good for one to be alone suggests that we cannot operate without friendship, support and love from other people. As social beings, married or single, we need each other. Our one main support may be gone, but we can reach out and find help from many others.

The third tendency is to throw oneself into creative activity, to produce something. The need to overcome loneliness often results in feverish rather than creative activity. In our deep fear of losing control and having to look at our loneliness, we often begin by filling up every hour of every day, so we have no time to think. Work on the job, at home and with volunteer organizations keeps us so worn out that we don't have time to grieve. We say yes to everyone who calls to ask for help, not realizing that we need time for ourselves, time to grieve and feel the pain, no matter how much it hurts.

Fromm's fourth classification — active loving — is the only real solution to loneliness. This loving is threefold: loving ourselves, loving God and loving others. Loving ourselves is the first step. If our self-esteem is low, if we think everyone else is better, or better-off than we are, if we have no confidence in our abilities and gifts, then we cannot love God or others.

Self-esteem

The answer to loneliness is within, in our sense of self-esteem and self-love. The word "self-love" sometimes is a warning flag for our conscience. Isn't it wrong to love yourself? Does the parental caution from your childhood, "Don't be selfish," prevent you from being comfortable with loving yourself? Many of us got the idea we were supposed to do away with concern for ourselves, get rid of our ego and be concerned only for others.

Genuine caring for ourselves, an awareness of our personal worth and a good sense of self-esteem are entirely different from egocentricity. The latter is a morbid preoccupation with ourselves and insensitivity to the needs of others. Excessive self-interest is the hallmark of a selfish person who is concerned with others only to the extent they can be of some use. Learning to know ourselves inside and out is the first step in learning to love ourselves. We must learn to recognize our "idiot" side — the one that always does things at inappropriate times or in stupid ways. We must become aware of sudden anger that lashes out at people around us, projecting some of our "dark side" on our neighbors. The part we dislike in others is often that part of ourselves that we do not like or understand. We must learn that there is a "murderer" within us that screams for revenge, anger and violence. There is also a caring side which wishes to give love and warmth. To truly love myself, I need to look at all of me, including the light and dark.

How do I learn to know myself?

1. By stopping and listening to my inmost self. This means finding time for solitude, silence and aloneness. Five to ten minutes in the quiet of the morning (or before retiring in the evening) gives me the time and space to listen to God's directions.

2. Journal-keeping has been an effective tool in examining my fears, anger and depression. I sort

out my thoughts, see how I can change and decide my course of action.

3. Fantasies and daydreams are clues to the inner self. On occasion I have used dream analysis to understand myself. Morton Kelsey's book *Dreams* has been a guide for me in this area.

4. A spiritual director, who will listen to my feelings, emotions, fears and actions and then give me options or ideas on how I can accomplish my goals, has been an invaluable help to me. Good spiritual directors do not give advice. They point the way to God but leave the decision up to me.

5. Physical exercise is an important tool in my search for self-esteem. Consistent exercise gives me the energy to clear up things that are bothering me. Brisk walking or the Red Cross-sponsored water-walking in our municipal swimming pool are my two favorites. Others prefer running, jogging, tennis or swimming.

After I begin to know myself, the next step is to take responsibility for what I find in myself. Taking charge, I pick a goal and work to make it the center of my life. I decide which of these elements — the dark, "idiot" murderer or the loving, caring individual — I want to express and which I do not choose to show. This focus helps me to become the loving person I want to be, because I have given some thought and prayer to the expression of that love.

As I became more comfortable with myself, I was able to reach out to others, forming new relationships and new friendships. At the same time my love of God grew because I slowly understood that God loves me with all my faults and failings. These are the other aspects of active loving, Fromm's fourth stage.

In my search for self-esteem I found many parts of myself that needed to be integrated and dealt with as a whole. I was searching for "wholeness" or "holiness." I am not pure spirit. I am not just rationality and consciousness, or just feelings, emotions and conditioned responses. I am body, soul, spirit and emotions all bound together. This is what God created me to be — a human being, not an angel or an animal. These various parts of me need to work together as a harmonious whole.

I cannot find this integrated whole by myself. I need my church — the fellowship of those who believe as I do. I need the friendship of Jesus Christ, who came as a human being with all the feelings and emotions that I have, who will walk with me as I make my journey. I need the support and love of people who have walked the path I am walking, those who understand that loneliness is part of our existence.

As we become more comfortable with our identity as a single person, we will reach out to relationships with other people and finally relationship with God.

We can learn from Thomas Merton: "The one who fears to be alone will never be anything but lonely, no matter how much he may surround himself with people. But the one who learns, in solitude and recollection, to be at peace with his own loneliness, and to prefer its reality to the illusion of merely natural companionship, comes to know the invisible companionship of God" (*Contemplative Prayer*).

_____ Five _____

Prayer

Zion was saying, "Yahweh has abandoned me,
    the Lord has forgotten me."
Can a woman forget her baby at the breast,
    feel no pity for the child she has borne?
Even if these were to forget,
    I shall not forget you.
Look, I have engraved you on the palms of my hands,
    your ramparts are ever before me (Is 49:14–16).

I complained as Zion did: "The Lord has abandoned me; my Lord has forgotten me." The world looked black and I could find no light. But Isaiah comforted me. "Can a mother forget her infant or be without tenderness for the child of her womb?" I knew I could not forget my nine babies. Even the three I miscarried are loved and cherished.

"Even should she forget, I will never forget you. See, upon the palms of my hands I have written your name. . . ." Isaiah promised that God our mother had not forgotten me. My creator would remember me always. I clung to that promise with both hands for the first few years of my widowhood. Prayer, my dialogue with God, was my lifesaver.

Why am I writing about prayer and spirituality? What does that have to do with grief? It is through our brokenness that we are open to finding God in a new and special way. Frequently the first time we hear God's voice in our lives is when we are at the bottom of a pit, unable to climb out by ourselves. We cry for help; God hears and answers us. This time we listen.

If we are novices at this praying business, we may need some guidelines. What is prayer? How do I pray? What do I say? Is there more than one kind of prayer?

There are almost as many definitions of prayer as there are ways of praying. The old faithful *Baltimore Catechism* axiom, "Prayer is the lifting up of the mind and heart to God," is a good one, if we remember that it is God who does the lifting, not us. Without God's initiative or grace we cannot pray. Thomas Green, S.J., says that even "the desire to pray is itself a clear sign of the Lord's presence. We cannot reach out to him unless he first draws us" (*Opening to God*).

Deep within us is a longing for God, a restlessness that says there is more to life than what is visible to us today. That longing prompts us to pray, expressing our anxieties, hopes, thanksgiving, sorrow, praise and petitions. If we have a desire to become closer to the Source of our being, then God is truly speaking and asking us to become more aware of the divine presence in our lives. How can we do this and still give enough time and energy to our families and work? God does not ask us to do the impossible. When it is time for us to take another step, God will give us the grace and opportunity to do so.

Finding Time for Prayer

"If I have to schedule one more thing in my busy day, I will lose my mind! My life is a mad rush. I simply can't add any more 'have-tos' to the 24 hours," I complained. So often we are caught up in our daily activities and we look at our schedules and say we haven't got time for prayer, yet the Hound of Heaven won't leave us alone.

How about praying while doing other things?

Are you chauffering kids back and forth several times a day as I did for so many years? That was a time I learned to say, "Lord, let me take a deep breath and see the beauty in these children as I bring them to their swimming lesson. Thank you for their good health that enables them to swim. Thank you for their energy and liveliness, even though it seems almost more than I can take." If it had been a wild day, I sometimes added: "Give me strength!" And God did.

Do you drive, participate in a car pool or take a train to work each day? You can take this time to open your heart to tell God how you feel: "Lord, it has been a mad rush this morning, but the sky is blue and the birds are singing. Thank you for a beautiful day." Or: "Lord, I'm sorry I was so irritable this morning. Help me so I won't bring this bad mood to the office. Let me see you in my co-workers."

Because we are a farm family, I often stand at the

window watching a good soaking rain come down on our fields and say, "Thank you, Lord." Sometimes the prayer is: "I don't see why you sent the rain just four miles away and didn't let any come on our fields. But, Lord, even though I don't understand your ways, I trust you will care for us."

Standing in line at the grocery counter or waiting for a place at the car wash provides me with a few minutes to tell God how my day is going and to listen to anything God might want to say.

None of this praying takes any block of time from busy schedules, but it can be the beginning of a dialogue with our Creator. As time goes by, we are more and more aware of God's presence, encountering our heavenly parent in our daily life.

Stairway to Heaven?

I had always looked on prayer as a ladder or staircase on which I moved up, step by step, rung by rung. Each litany, rosary or memorized formal prayer brought me closer to God. The more I said, the closer I got, and if I did it all correctly, I would be rewarded by a spiritual experience or insight into God's love.

I was wrong. Prayer is much more than that. It is not something I *do* at certain times of the day. It is a bringing of myself into the presence of God through all my actions, inactions, thoughts and words, and letting God take over from there. I do this by listening to God in the word, in liturgy and in my life. St. Benedict perceives prayer as an habitual awareness of God's presence in our lives and a willingness to conform to what God wants. For me, prayer is a letting go of self, listening within to God's word, and following God's will in my actions.

70

100 Ways to Pray

I once attended a workshop where the speaker's topic was "100 Ways to Pray." We laughed, but she was not exaggerating! There are as many ways to pray as there are people. Not only do we each have our own way of finding God, but at different times in our life we need different types of prayer.

Spending an hour each day praying before the Blessed Sacrament is great, but not too practical for those of us who hold down jobs, keep a home in running order and raise children. In the middle of the grief process, it is difficult to focus on anything for a whole hour — especially prayer. Even when our families have left the nest, we have more demands than ever as worker, homemaker, volunteer and sometime baby sitter of grandchildren. But is prayer only spending time on your knees? Not at all. We are not contemplative nuns or monks, just ordinary people trying to know our Lord better.

Familiar prayers — like the Our Father, the Hail Mary, the rosary — have a definite place in our lives, especially when we find it difficult to pray. But don't limit yourself to those. Reach out to different types of prayer.

I open myself to God by sitting quietly in the morning and repeating the Jesus Prayer, relaxing my mind and body and spirit. I do the same by joining in the rosary our parish says before each daily liturgy. An offering of my day to God as I get breakfast sets the tone for the day.

Seeing Christ present in your children as they go through the routines, disagreements and emergencies in leaving for school can initiate a spontaneous

71

prayer of thankfulness: "Thanks, God, for getting them out of the door this morning while we are still speaking to each other!"

Seeing Christ's presence in my elderly neighbor when she asks me to pick up a quart of milk for her and I have a hundred other things to do that morning can elicit a prayer: "You always had time for everyone, Lord. Help me to follow your way."

Prayer is taking time to listen to someone who is hurting and saying to them, "I am here. I will be with you as you hurt and we will walk together." In making myself present to another, I am making myself present to God.

We can see God through things. Since God does not have a human body, we can't touch, hear or see the divine presence directly. But through God's actions in our lives and in the world of creation we are conscious of that presence.

A prayer can be inspired by looking at a new calcite crystal for my collection or watching the goldfinches swinging on the feeder outside my window, marveling at the color and beauty of God's creation. Pick some object you enjoy — a flower, candle, leaf, stone. Place it in front of you. Look at it as if you were seeing it for the first time — its color, shape, size and shadow. If your mind wanders (and it will), bring yourself back to the loveliness that is there. Where does the loveliness come from?

Dishwashing is a mundane task that doesn't take too much concentration, so I pray as I stand at the sink. I focus on the dish I am cleaning, the beauty, the line, the clay or metal. Holding a dirty pan in my hands I thank God for the raw materials creation has provided, for the miners who risked their lives to make the minerals accessible, for the people who stood in an assembly line to make the pan, for the salesperson who sold it to me. This can be an occasion to breathe a prayer of thanks for those unknown people who make my life easier: "Thanks for this pan, Lord. Watch over and care for all those who had any part in fashioning it."

Do you ever turn on a special record or tape and listen to the words and the music? Take a comfortable position, ask God to help you hear it in relation to the divine will in creation, and immerse yourself in the sound. What does God say to you in this music? How does it relate to your life? You are opening yourself to God's presence, giving your Lord the time and space to speak to you.

Father William McNamara, a Carmelite monk and spiritual writer, encourages us to use almost any human experience — watching a good TV show, having dinner with a close friend, listening to music, reading a book — as the basis for prayer and reflection. We must become aware of God and make each encounter with creation a time of encounter with God.

When I was young, I knew that all priests and sisters said the *Divine Office*. I thought that was something reserved exclusively for them; we lay people didn't have time — or weren't good enough — to do that. But recently there have been many books published with selections from the *Liturgy of the Hours* or the *Divine Office* so we can join our prayers morning and evening with those in the monastery, cloister or convent. We can be part of the universal church, offering our prayers as a community.

One of my most profound experiences of prayer was visiting L'Orangerie Museum in Paris where the impressionist masterpiece *Water Lilies* is displayed. God's hand in Claude Monet's life was so evident in these paintings that for the first time I realized the gift of truly great artists — that of making you aware of God's presence within yourself.

Prayer is more than seeing God in created things. Prayer is about life experiences. We need to get close to our center through the events in our life. The 6:00 o'clock news, a disagreement with your sister, a tragic newspaper headline, an illness, an award that your child won in school — whatever is a part of your life belongs in your prayer.

Prayer of Tears

Crying, when we lose control over our emotions, can be a form of prayer. God is also beyond our control. Tears force us to remember that we are creatures. Letting the tears flow is letting go of the control of our lives, letting God take over.

I learned to give myself a special time to grieve. Often I would put supper on the table for the children, excuse myself, go upstairs to my bedroom, shut the door and cry. Father Edward Hays says that "crying is an honest and an incarnational or bodily prayer that reaches the ear and heart of God. . . . Tears are the prayer beads of us all — men and women — because they arise from the fullness of the heart" ("The Prayer of Tears," *Sign*, Oct. 1979). In that case I sent thousands of prayers to the ear and heart of God.

After 15 or 20 minutes, when I had the tears all out of my system, I could go back downstairs and finish my meal. Having told God of my hurt and pain, I knew I would get help to go on. God heard the prayer of tears that flowed from my heart with a speed that reminds us of a parent hearing the tears of a child. As mother, I answer my children's tears. As mother and father, God answered my tears in the same manner.

Prayer is listening. It is taking time to find space and solitude in my life and learning to empty myself so I can be open to God's word in my life. I offer myself to others when I listen to them. I offer myself to God when I listen to God.

Prayer is being a peacemaker. I often think of the times I have been a family peacemaker over the years, and I realize that my efforts are a prayer, an attempt to bring God's joy and love into our family life.

Keeping a journal can be a prayer when you ask God to help you with your decisions. Write a letter to Jesus; ask for a reply. Sometimes you will find yourself writing down his answer to you. If you have difficulty with a relationship, carry on an imaginary conversation with that person in your journal. Let the other person enter the conversation. That will help in sorting out your difficulties and give you some insights into your problem. Ask Jesus what he wants to say to both of you and write that down also.

Scripture

Scripture reading is a special encounter with God. It is the web which interconnects all the facets of my prayer life. Daily Bible reading has proved to be a network which pulls together all the ways I pray and leads me to the presence of God. Books written especially for beginners started me in serious, disciplined prayer. They showed me a variety of ways to slow down my mind and body and to reach out to God.

Psalms speak powerfully to those who are hurting and in pain. They are Israel's prayer journal and, as such, can help us in our journey.

It is important not only to read but also to meditate on what the word of God is saying to you. Put yourself in one of the gospel stories. Imagine you are a soldier at the foot of the cross, or one of the crowd where Jesus fed the five thousand. Meditate on it. Use your imagination, your intellect and finally your will to apply it to your life. What does all this say to you? What does Jesus want you to do? How must you change?

Prayer and Change

Emilie Griffin says that prayer is a very dangerous business. "For all the benefits it offers of growing closer to God, it carries with it one great element of risk: the possibility of change. In prayer we open ourselves to the chance that God will do something with us that we had not intended!" (*Clinging*).

Ten years ago, that statement would have scared me. After all, I knew who I was! Why should I want to step into the unknown? I was afraid to change, afraid of risks. I might be rebuffed, confronted or even fail! It took me a while before I was comfortable with the fact that it was O.K. to fail, O.K. to be human. Falling short of my goals and expectations is not wrong. If I allow failure to discourage me, keeping me anxious and depressed most of the time, then I am wrong. The positive aspect of failure is that it can be a learning experience and an incentive for growth.

Remember, in my early grieving for my husband, I said I asked God to find me a man? Never in my wildest dreams did I think of asking for a closer relationship with God. I wanted a relationship with a man, but my Creator saw I was not ready for that. Instead, God opened up ways for me to go to college full time (not just one or two courses a semester), change majors (from elementary education to theology), and reach out to help others who were grieving from the loss of a spouse. God knew I needed to find out who I was and who God is. By listening to others I would learn more about myself and my relationship with God.

Slowly but surely I took one small step and then another, trusting that God knew my true needs better than I did. Each step has given me the courage to try a bigger one next time. During that process my children became more aware of who God had created them to be and what their abilities are. Each one is developing a special, unique relationship with their Creator. I have changed and so have they.

Taking 20 minutes twice a day for centering or contemplative prayer has helped slow down my lifestyle, reduce tension and stress and hear God's voice in solitude and peace. There have been many excellent books written on this type of prayer. A bibliography in the appendix includes those I found helpful, although it is by no means complete.

This chapter has touched on some of the ways I pray. Certainly I did not use all these ways at once. Different times in my life have called for different types of prayer. By listening to God's word within, I moved from one type to another as God guided me.

You will find that some of my ways are helpful and some are not. That's fine. They are meant to stimulate you and get you started on your journey. Each one of us has his or her own walk with God.

Bereavement was a learning experience when I opened my heart and let God in. The question is: "Do I want to spend the rest of my life grieving, mourning the loss of my love, and feeling sorry for myself, or do I want to move through the pain, close the door gently on the past, learn to enjoy the present moment and look forward to the future?"

Six.

Tender Loving Care

God saw everything he had made, and indeed
it was very good (Gn 1:31).

God created me a beautiful person, but during my grieving process I wasn't so sure. I knew I
should take good care of my body, but oh! it is so
hard those first few months. It took all of my energy
just to get out of bed in the morning, let alone think
about proper nutrition, sleep, relaxation and exercise.

My recommendation is to read this chapter and
choose just one idea a week and make it part of your
routine. If you can't incorporate it into your life in
that short time, continue on the same path for another week. There is no **definite** timetable. Trying to
do everything at once will only discourage you. Slow-

ly but surely you will find your energy and vitality returning.

Good Nutrition

Because I had nine growing children at home when Jim died, including several teenagers, it was imperative that I fix well-balanced meals for all of us. Adequate amounts of milk, meat, fruits, vegetables and grains are important allies in recovering from the intense stages of grief and preventing illness. It is very easy to fix a frozen pizza or rely on fast foods, but it does not provide the nutritional balance that is necessary especially during times of stress.

The diagnosis of Jim's diabetes had changed our eating habits many years before any of the children were born. Jim and I had learned to avoid the butter, cream and sweets that had been part of a farm family's meals for generations. As the children became active in the 4-H program, our awareness of good nutrition helped all of us to maintain better health. Science moves at a fast pace making it important to stay current with the latest discoveries.

A recent publication by the American Medical Association warns that we must be conscious of our need for vitamins, minerals, fiber, proteins, carbohydrates and fat. Vitamins are complex organic substances found in most foods, although a few are synthesized within the body. They are needed in small amounts to regulate metabolism, speed normal growth and assist in the functioning of the body. Minerals, needed in minute amounts, are also essential to bodily functioning. Like vitamins, they come from outside sources. Vegetables, fruit and milk products are especially good sources of both vitamins and minerals.

Fiber or roughage is found in unrefined flour, cereals, fruit, leafy vegetables and legumes. Known to aid intestinal digestion, absorption and elimination, it may also help prevent digestive problems and cancer of the large intestine. Studies have indicated that fiber affects the way the body uses fat and therefore may be helpful in reducing deposits of fatty tissue that can lead to atherosclerosis or hardening of the arteries. Protein is found in two forms; meat, fish, eggs, milk and cheese provide animal protein, while peas, beans and other legumes are important sources of vegetable protein. Both types provide amino acids used for growth and repair of body tissue.

Carbohydrates, contrary to popular belief, are not the "bad guys" of the nutrition world. By providing fuel for the body, they see that we have enough energy for the brain, which, ounce for ounce, needs more fuel than any other organ. Cereals, breads, pasta, potatoes and sugar are the most common suppliers of this important nutrient.

Fat should be consumed in limited quantities, although avoiding it completely is not recommended. It is needed to maintain the sheathing that covers nerves and in the tissue that insulates our bodies as well as aiding in the absorption of vitamins A, D, E and K. Saturated fat comes from meat and dairy products; unsaturated fat is found in margarine and different types of vegetable oils.

Food experts recommend the following daily consumption of the four food groups for adults:

• Two or more cups of milk and milk products (including yogurt, cheese and ice cream);

• Two or more servings of meat (including red meat, fish, poultry and eggs, dried beans and nuts);

- Four or more servings of fruits and vegetables;
- Four or more servings of cereals and breads (including rice and pasta).

A well-rounded diet including these groups ensures that you are receiving the 47 nutrients necessary for optimum energy level.

As I moved toward my 60th birthday, I had trouble maintaining my proper weight. The pointer on the scale kept creeping upward. My body still required the same amount of nutrients as before, but since my metabolism had slowed down and physical activity had decreased, I did not need the same number of calories. This again required changing my eating habits to maintain good health.

My twin aunts, Mildred and Maude, had lived together for 78 years, longer than most married couples, when Maude died. As one of her last wishes, Maude asked her sister to promise she would fix herself one hot meal a day when she was alone. Many times that pledge was the only incentive Mildred had to cook a well-balanced, hot meal for herself. A few years ago she astounded the doctor with her fast recovery from a broken hip. Within six months this 85-year-old lady was walking her usual 10 to 15 blocks a day. Good nutrition and daily exercise had speeded the healing process. The four food groups are still part of her daily routine.

Fluids

An adequate fluid intake is important during mourning. Glen Davidson, in his book, *Understanding Mourning*, recommends that we drink more fluids than we feel we need. Sluggishness, "thick tongues," tightness of the throat and reduced appetite can often be traced to a lack of fluids.

Choosing the right drink is important. Several glasses of water or fruit juice during the day provide enough fluid for moderate activity, although increased amounts are necessary during extra activity or hot weather. Alcohol and drinks containing caffeine should be used sparingly.

Most of us are conscious that we can consume too much caffeine in coffee but are not always aware that there may be other sources of caffeine in our daily diet. Tea, chocolate, baked goods, frozen dairy products, gelatins, puddings and soft candies are culprits. Colas and some other soft drinks are also on top of the list.

Caffeine is an ingredient in more than a thousand prescription and over-the-counter drugs: weight control aids, alertness tablets, asthma medications, pain relief tablets, diuretics and cold/allergy remedies. A few years ago I was jumpy, easily irritated and found it difficult to sleep at night. The doctor's advice, to cut back on the amount of coffee I drank, took care of my problem.

Learning to be a label reader for foods and medications can make us aware of what we are consuming. This is an important step in helping our body recover from the shock of grief.

Illness and Disease

"I'm so exhausted tonight that I can't think straight."

"I'm too tired to get up this morning."

"I have been having trouble sleeping at night. I just get up and wander around or read a book."

"Our whole family has had one cold after another this winter."

"My back has gone out again! My whole body
seems to be deteriorating!"

All of these complaints cropped up in my life
during the first years after Jim's death. Mourners do
not realize that they are especially vulnerable to disease and illness during the grieving process. Right
after Jim died, my mother cautioned me: "Expect that
you or the children will come down with an illness or
there will be a rash of broken bones." She was right.
We didn't have any broken bones, but we sure did
have illnesses.

Within three months 2-year-old Jennifer was in
the hospital with pneumonia and asthma. Steve, the
3-year-old, followed her the next week. In fact, one or
the other of the children was hospitalized every fall
for the next two years. A continual round of upper
respiratory infections, earaches and allergies spread
through the family during the next months. Our defenses had been weakened, allowing viruses to get a
good hold on us.

What can we do to keep ourselves in shape during
this period of mourning so that illness does not get the
best of us? Authorities recommend several steps.

The first one is to be aware that shock, which
affects our body, mind, emotions and spirit, dazes and
weakens us for a while. My mother knew this. Very
likely her German mother and grandmother knew it
also. Only now are psychologists and doctors using
scientific studies to prove what people knew all along:
After death a family will very likely be prone to illness
or accidents.

The first few years after Jim died I kept busy for

every hour of every day. If I wasn't occupied fixing meals, sewing clothes, cleaning the house or going to some child's school activity, I was helping with church and service organizations. Volunteering for every organization possible kept me from thinking about my loss (a form of denial), but that only postponed the inevitable. The toll began to show, and I soon found myself battling high blood pressure. Stress had weakened my body.

Slowing down, choosing a moderate amount of activity and keeping a simple lifestyle alleviated some of the physical and mental stress. Symptoms of grief do pop up in unexpected places.

Exercise

The importance of daily exercise for the newly widowed cannot be overemphasized, even though the last thing we want to do is add more physical activities to our daily routine. Recent scientific studies show that regular exercise stimulates chemicals in the brain which in turn eliminate depression, making us happier and more alert. The American Medical Association recommends three 20-minute sessions of vigorous activity weekly. In addition to the usual suggestions of walking, running, swimming, tennis and bicycling, they include garden work in their list. For many people, gardening is more than exercise; it is a labor of love that helps them slow down and reduce tension in their lives.

Running, aerobics and tennis are popular forms of exercise, but again, the second guidepost from Chapter 2 comes in handy: Be gentle with yourself. Emotional grief work is physically exhausting. Don't add strenuous exercise when your body is already vulnerable. A walk early in the morning or late in the evening several times a week is a good way to start. As your body adjusts to the new activity, pick up your pace and raise your goals.

I have never learned to swim, but recently I found an activity I have learned to love — water-walking. Four or five times a week, I walk laps in a swimming pool, nine laps for every quarter of a mile. At the end of 10 miles the Red Cross recognized my achievement with a patch for my swimsuit. More important than the patch, however, is the feeling of energy and well-being that has come from a regular exercise routine. Those 20-minute walks give me time to clear the cobwebs from my brain, look at my goals and talk with God about what I am being asked to do. I come home relaxed and usually in a much better frame of mind.

The A.M.A. also recommends that you consult your physican before beginning *any* exercise program if you are:

- Over 60
- Over 45 and unaccustomed to vigorous activity
- A heavy smoker (more than 20 cigarettes a day)
- Overweight
- Afflicted with any long-term health problem, such as heart or kidney disorders or high blood pressure.
- In poor physical condition to start with.

Sleep (Or Lack Thereof)

Like most widows and widowers, I had trouble getting to sleep at night. Being alone in our king-sized bed emphasized the terrible loneliness that assailed me at night. In order to ignore that loneliness, I would plan my next day's activities. That was no solution. There were so many items on that list in my head that I couldn't relax. Here are a few remedies that worked for me.

1. Cut back on drinks with caffeine.
2. Exercise daily.
3. Keep a book handy and read until your eyelids grow heavy.
4. Have a cup of herb tea to relax tired muscles and an active mind.
5. Try a hot, soaking bath to relax muscles.
6. Take time to unwind before going to bed: watch TV (not a horror show), read, meditate or pray.
7. Write thoughts, hopes and dreams in a journal.
8. Write down a list of things to do the next day. (This keeps them from running around in your head.)

If at all possible, stay away from sleeping pills. The National Academy of Science's Institute of Medicine says that these medicines have a cumulative effect. If you take them for a week, there is four to six times more in your bloodstream on day seven than there was on day one. Be sure to consult your doctor about any long-term use.

Again I suggest that "Be gentle with yourself" is an important guidepost in this area of physical well-being. "One Day at a Time," the byword for Alcoholics Anonymous, is a good motto for all of us.

_____Seven_____

Financial Headaches

For a while after a spouse's death, there are numerous things to be taken care of: letters, thank-you notes, banks, savings and loans, credit unions, life insurance, fraternal order benefits, Social Security, veterans' benefits, lawyers, estate administration, health insurance, financial investments, paper sorting, state and national income tax. There are not enough hours in the day to accomplish all that "has" to be done! Where do we begin? How do we cope?

Grief work (both conscious and unconscious) takes up much energy. Again, be gentle with yourself! Take care of no more than one financial problem a day.

How you deal with these problems depends to some extent on your earlier financial experience. If you are a husband or wife who routinely did all the book work, this may be no headache at all. If you are a parent who has a job outside the home, your biggest problem may be to find time for anything except working, cooking and spending time with the children.

If you are a mother who stays home with the children, perhaps the biggest difficulty is trying to decide which area to work at first. Since I was a mother at home, I got caught up in the day-to-day routine, never finding the energy to tackle the financial problems that loomed in front of me. As a newly widowed person I needed stimulation outside the four walls of my house. It took some time before I found the courage to reach out and ask for help.

Breaking down the problem list into priorities was my first step in removing the stress of over-programmed days. A paper entitled "Jobs to Do List" (Ag Plus Software) straightened out my thinking. The list is divided into three sections: A-high priority, B-get done when convenient, C-low priority. Taking each of the jobs mentioned above and putting it into the proper category helped me to be more realistic and decide which item to take care of first.

Under "high priority" I put "time for myself" as number one. Running from one place to another for 18 hours a day, it was easy to avoid my prime responsibility — grief work. As I said before, allowing one-half hour a day to feel the pain, acknowledge the hurt, and cry by yourself and with your children can prevent the tears from flowing in inappropriate places like the middle of the grocery store or during church services. "Time for recreation and play" should also be on the top of your priority list. No matter how many important things need to be done, take time to let go and relax.

Attorneys

As far as financial and legal matters are concerned, probably the highest priority items are making an appointment with your lawyer and contacting the Social Security office.

My first step was to call for an appointment with my attorney. Since loss and grief was uppermost in my mind and I was unable to think logically those first months, competent advice from my family lawyer and help from a knowledgeable friend were wise investments. The attorney filed my husband's will, made an appointment for me at the Social Security office, helped me to apply for life insurance benefits, checked on my income tax status and made sure payments and/or estimates were up-to-date. The friend reminded me of financial and tax deadlines that I might have overlooked.

Your lawyer will need to see insurance policies (life, health, car, homeowner's), files, tax records, tax returns and check stubs at your first appointment. Bring a certified copy of the death certificate for each insurance policy so that application may be made for benefits. These papers are issued at the County Court House if your funeral director has not taken care of that item for you. If you have automatic withdrawals from your bank account for an insurance policy, the attorney should check and see that agreement is now cancelled. It might be a wise idea to double check with your insurance agent to make sure you have all outstanding policies.

Attorney fees are calculated two ways: on a percentage of the estate or by the hour. Which way you choose depends mainly on the size of the estate. Discussing attorney fees at the first appointment can relieve anxiety about the cost.

Each state has its own laws concerning the filing of a will and probate of an estate. Even if there is no will, the court has to be notified of the death. Depending on the size of the estate, probate can be simple or complex. My attorney warned me that the court usually does not permit probate to be settled in less than a year, tying up some of the assets for at least that long. His assistance in dealing with legal and financial issues gave me a sense of control in this vitally important area. Step by step I learned to take care of them without Jim.

Financial Confidence

One financial planner said the most important thing a widow or widower can do is to ask questions — over and over again if necessary. "Don't be embarrassed to ask for explanations. People who make mistakes are those who don't ask," he warned.

If you don't understand your spouse's stock brokerage account statement, ask your attorney. If you still don't understand, ask the firm's account executive. Ask three, four or five times. You can learn!

If you don't agree with your attorney's recommendations, get a second opinion. Don't rush. There is plenty of time.

Widows might have a special set of questions that they wish to ask themselves after a period of time.

"Am I happy with the attorney I have? Do I trust him or her?" If he was your spouse's advisor and they were able to communicate well, it does not necessarily mean that you are comfortable with that arrangement. If you are a woman, you might ask yourself, "Would I be happier with an attorney who is a woman?"

The important thing to look for is not the sex of the attorney, but the rapport, trust and confidence you have in him or her. You owe it to yourself to find someone who can talk with you on your level and be willing to explain the process to you even if it has to be explained many times. Good communication skills in attorneys, bankers, insurance agents and financial planners can make this experience not one to be dreaded but one that is a source of growth and learning.

Changing attorneys is not a step that should be taken right away. Perhaps putting it on our low-priority list and letting the idea germinate for a while will help straighten out the mixed-up thinking that we experience at first.

Death Benefits

The Social Security office was my second stop. Death benefits should be applied for promptly. The employees are well-qualified and experienced in helping newly widowed people.

If your spouse has been receiving a Social Security check, remember not to cash the one that arrives after the death. It should be returned immediately. If in doubt, contact your Social Security office. The toll free telephone number is in the phone book.

Don't forget death benefits from Veterans' Administration, railroad or company pensions. Fraternal orders (Knights of Columbus, Lutheran Brotherhood, Elks, etc.) as sources of death benefits are often overlooked.

Banking Information

Although most of us are aware that safety deposit boxes are sealed at the time of death, it can be an unpleasant surprise to find that joint bank accounts are also automatically closed. A request can be made for the bank to release those funds. Usually a new account is established to handle money received after death. A letter of appointment from the court is necessary to start this new account.

It is possible to be without money from the original account for a short period of time. Don't let this bring on a panic attack. A short term loan can be arranged to tide you over for a few months. Established customer service departments in banks, savings and loans and credit unions can give information on loans, interest rates, health, accident and death coverage. Although borrowing money was a new and scary proposition for me, counseling and advice from a loan officer relieved my apprehension and restored my confidence. Another hurdle conquered!

If a bank was named as executor of the estate and/or a trust was set up, you can rely on the bank trust department to help you with any questions or problems. Most of the time the trust officer is also an attorney who is skilled in working with grieving widows and widowers.

Perhaps your spouse designated you as executor or administrator of the estate. It may be that you are highly qualified in this area and have no worries about your ability to handle the work. If you feel that the responsibility is too great, you can ask the court to appoint someone else to act in your place. A bank is usually a good, neutral party to work with all members of the family at a time when emotions are running high.

Health Insurance

Neglect checking on health insurance at your own risk! If you were covered under your spouse's employment policy, very likely your benefits will end, either immediately or within a given period of time. Deciding whether to continue with the same insurance, choosing another individual or group plan, moving to a Health Maintenance Organization (HMO), or adding a major medical plan can add much tension to your life.

Help in choosing the best type of family health insurance can reduce this stress to a manageable level. Take plenty of time to search out the agencies, companies and hospitals that can aid you in this vital decision. Insurance companies often provide booklets that explain in understandable language the different kinds of health protection to help you make an informed decision. Libraries are also a good source with librarians ready and willing to assist you in finding information. Banks frequently have one-day seminars to help you sort out the latest health insurance information.

Many hospitals in conjunction with area Agencies on Aging are now offering free health insurance advice as part of their educational and outreach programs. Lorraine Stedman, a health insurance advocate for Iowa Area IV Agency on Aging, says her services are tailored to individual needs. They include evaluation of existing policies, unbiased counseling regarding Medicare Supplement insurance and long-term care policies, assisting with Medicare claims review and appeal processes and helping to resolve health insurance complaints. Newsletters and seminars keep the client up-to-date on recent changes in the health insurance field. These health care advocates are available in both urban and rural areas. Inquire at your nearest hospital.

In addition, hospitals have added Medicare counseling for patients and their families. These full-time employees go through medical bills, distinguish just what services were rendered, file supplemental insurance and then check up and see if the money was collected. They also help the patient file for a review if the claim was denied. Since most doctors have discontinued filing the insurance claims for their patients, this free service by the hospital makes sure you are receiving all entitled benefits.

Financial Planners and Investment Advisers

Investment and financial planning is another area that frequently kept me awake at night. I felt especially incompetent in this area. Again it is important to go to the right person for help. How do we know where to go? Learning the difference between financial planners, investment advisers, stock brokers and insurance advisers helps us to take that first step with more confidence.

"Financial planner" and "investment adviser" are not necessarily synonymous terms. Financial planners examine your entire financial situation and work out a long-term plan for money management, including budgeting, savings, insurance and payment of loans. They receive compensation in the form of an annual set fee, depending on the size of your estate.

Investment advisers select individual securities, stocks and bonds in keeping with your investment goals. They are not affiliated with investment firms and do not receive commissions for the buying and selling of securities. Fees are based on a percentage of the money turned over to them for investment management.

On top of that, there are insurance people, bankers and stock brokers, all of whom are anxious to advise you on the investment of your money since they receive a percentage of the money involved. The important thing is to find someone you can trust. Ask your friends if they have invested any money and how they went about it. Your attorney may be able to recommend someone. Go to the library and look up a list of Certified Financial Planners. These people have passed a series of rigorous examinations and are subject to an annual review by the International Board of Standards and Practices for Certified Financial Planners, Inc. (IBCFP). This board encourages continuing education and enforces a strict Code of Ethics.

Job, School and Career Planning

Very likely investment is the least of our problems! Several areas take precedence over the investment of money: "Now that I have only my income to support us, will we be able to make it?" "Can I find a job that will pay enough to hire a baby sitter and support us too?" "Do I have to go back to school and get more education?"

Again the recommendation of guidepost No. 1 is a good one to follow. Don't be in a hurry to make changes. When you do feel ready to take steps to move on there is a lot of help available.

Community colleges, universities, job service and employment agencies are great sources of information on the types of jobs available and career planning assistance. The nationwide program, Displaced Homemakers Network, gives much help to those venturing into the job market for the first time.

If the thought of going back to school scares you, or you feel it is too expensive, make an appointment with the director of continuing education at a nearby college or technical school. Students over 22 years of age who have never previously enrolled in college often qualify for special financial aid. Even if you have some education behind you, there are many loans, grants and scholarships earmarked for the non-traditional student. Although there were no grants available when I decided to return to school, taking one course and passing it gave me the self-confidence to continue. By the time I was ready to become a full-time student, the private college I had chosen granted me a tuition scholarship.

ACCEL (Academic Credit for College Equivalent Learning), evening courses in nearby cities, and weekend college programs are all innovations that have sprung up to accommodate the returning college student. According to Quentin H. Gessner of the University of Nebraska-Lincoln, "The explosion of knowledge, the increasing complexity of life, the advancements in technology, the creation of new jobs and the displacement of others, a longer life expectancy and instantaneous communication technologies are indicators of a changing world" (*Handbook on Continuing Education*). In this changing world adult learners need to take advantage of career and development counseling that is offered by colleges, universities and technical schools. Career counselors give personality and career inventories, show students how their abilities and gifts are suited for certain types of work and advise them in applying for jobs. They are up-to-date on current and future trends and can see areas that will be looking for graduates to fill their needs.

In the back of this book there is a bibliography which might be helpful in directing you to appropriate books, groups and organizations.

Guidepost No. 6, "Just for Today," had to be brought out again and again. I had to learn that not everything needed to be accomplished in one day, one week or even one month. When I went to bed at night, I reviewed all my accomplishments of the day, even though some days I seemed to make very little progress. Thanking God for what had been done, giving up the burden for the night and telling God I would work on it again tomorrow relieved my anxiety. A good night's sleep made the list look smaller in the morning.

_____Eight_____

Children and Death

No one ever told me that grief felt so like fear
(C.S. Lewis).

C.S. Lewis, in his classic, *A Grief Observed*, has
given us a clue to understanding our children's grief.
Fear of the unknown is a problem for adults, but even
more so for a child who is not able to draw on pre-
vious life experiences.

"Will Mom be able to support us like Daddy
did?"

"What will happen to me if Mom (Dad) dies
too?"

"How will Daddy ever raise us alone?"

"Suppose Mom gets married again and I don't
like him."

"Will we have to move?"

101

Unspoken fears not only contribute to stress and tension in family life, but they can wreck havoc years later when new relationships appear on the scene.

I made many mistakes those first years. One daughter told me recently that she regrets how we acted as if everything was normal, because it was not. I agree with her. Our life was not the same, but I tried to make it seem that way. I can remember thinking that if I fell apart, then all nine children would also go to pieces. I didn't think I could cope with ten crying people. I avoided looking at my own emotions and hoped that by modeling I could show the children how to control the expression of their grief. This was mistake number one. We (children and parents alike) need to cry and express our sorrow verbally to a good listener. Only then can any of us let go.

I was so busy dealing with my own grief, I did not look out and see how it was affecting the individual children. As I noted previously, they followed my example as I had hoped, but since I supressed outward expressions of my grief, they did the same. As a result they dealt with unresolved feelings and suppressed emotions years later as they matured and left home.

As soon as I admitted that I was afraid — of the future, of lack of security, of the sheer magnitude of the job ahead — I started on my road to recovery. In reaching down inside, acknowledging my fears and sharing this new-found knowledge with them, I gave them permission to articulate their own fears and questions and start on their own road to recovery. As I have grown and shared with them just how I am coping with the changes in my life, they follow my example and work through grief at their own pace.

The stages of grief — denial, anger, bargaining, depression and acceptance — are very real for children as well as adults.

Denial

As with adults, children need time to absorb the shock when a father or mother dies. A parent is *the* source of their security. When the foundation of their life disappears, fear builds up walls that take a long time to tumble down. We may be thrown off track by a child's actions. She may say, "Oh!" when told of a parent's death and then run out to play with friends. This is denial at work and we must allow her time to absorb the earth-shattering news. She simply may not have heard what was said. Any parent or teacher will tell you that children do not learn the first time they hear or see something. It has to be repeated many times in different ways for it to penetrate. It is up to the parent to create a comfortable environment where the child will be able to cry, ask questions and voice his or her fears.

"Why did God take my mommy away?"

"Was it because she was bad and God wanted to punish her?"

"Was it because I was bad and God is punishing me?"

"What if you die? What will happen to me?"

"Who will take care of me? Will I be an orphan?"

Honesty and truthfulness are the watchwords when dealing with denial. To the best of our ability we have to tell our children how we are looking at the future at this moment. There will be times that we have to say, "I don't know," followed by a reassuring, "but I am going to learn."

We need to use exact words, not euphemisms such as:

"He has gone on a long journey." (Will there be a resurgence of fears when you go on a trip next year?)

"She has gone to heaven." (What and where is heaven?)

"Mommy passed away." (Passed away into what?)

"Daddy is asleep." (Will I die when I sleep too?)

Again, honesty and truthfulness, not evasions and half-truths, are the way to a closer relationship, no matter how difficult it is to voice the words: "Your daddy died. I can hardly believe it myself. Every time I start to talk about it I cry. I know you must feel the same way, so let's cry together right now. There are going to be lots of decisions for me to make in the next few days, but when the funeral is over and things have settled down, we will spend some good time together and talk about it some more. For right now, how about a good hug?"

Your words will vary depending on the age of the child. The important thing is not the words you use. Acknowledging your feelings and allowing them to acknowledge theirs will open lines of communication that help in the healing process for child and parent alike.

Children and Anger

Anger takes many forms.

"Mom is never around when I need to talk to her. She is so busy working she hasn't got time for me."

"Mom and Dad had a big fight a few days before he died. It is all her fault."

104

"Mom has been dating this man. I don't want another dad." "Daddy's always at work and we have to go to a baby sitter." "Why does everything have to change? Mommy had to go to work when Daddy died and isn't there when I come home."

Children get a double message from us when it comes to expressing anger. We tell them it is wrong to be angry. We correct them when they scream, yell and pick fights with siblings or schoolmates, as of course we should, but we fail to give them an acceptable outlet for those emotions. What are they going to do with those angry feelings? If they are not able to express anger to us, they will have to express them someplace. Screaming, yelling, picking fights, sometimes even hitting because of their frustration are the result of holding in those emotions. The opposite reaction — being extra good and obedient — can also be a sign that feelings are being suppressed. Again we have to remind them — and ourselves: Feelings are not right or wrong. They just are. It is what we do with those feelings that can be right or wrong. We need to allow our children to say to us:

"I'm angry at God. He took my mother away."

"I'm really mad at Daddy. He left me when I loved him so much."

"I'm scared that if I am bad, God will take you away from me too."

Sometimes we need to make those statements ourselves, and prefix them with: "Do you sometimes feel this way?" Allow the children to unload their fears and concerns on you, or encourage them to talk to a good friend of the family. Older children can be encouraged to keep a journal of their feelings. Assure them it is theirs alone and no one else will read it.

Privacy is very important during the adolescent and teen years.

Sometimes the oldest son or daughter starts to fill in for the absent parent. Some people actually say something like:

"Now that your dad is gone you will have to be the man of the house."

"As the oldest daughter, you will have to take over running the house in place of your mother."

"Now that your dad is gone, you be a special help to your mother."

The stress and pressure put on young people, even in their teen years, is unbelievable. No one can take the place of a beloved father or mother. A child or adolescent does not know it is futile to try and will attempt the impossible. Frequently anger builds up inside because of the pressures and the child will lash out in entirely inappropriate ways or even become ill trying to ease the parent's pain. Much trouble can be avoided if the parent assures the child the family will all work together.

Mothers or fathers themselves cannot assume both female and male roles. They may have to enlarge their areas of expertise, giving consideration to a male or female point of view, but they can never replace the absent spouse.

Make sure your message is heard. When Jim died, many well-meaning people said to Dan, my oldest son, "Now you will have to be the man of the family." He was 16 years old. I remember distinctly sitting down and saying to him that those people were mistaken. He did not have to be, nor could he be, "the man of the family." Today he has no memory of our conversation. He did take on much responsibility for the younger children and had to work through some of his anger years later. One telling was not enough.

Children and Bargaining

"Dear God, I will be good and never do anything wrong again. Please let my daddy come back to me!"

"Dear God, I will help Mom around the house, never fight with my brothers and sisters, get good grades in school — and you take away this awful hurt inside me."

Children are no different than we are when it comes to bargaining with God. Life has taught them that everything operates under cause and effect. When their actions are good, they are praised by their parents. When they do something bad, they are punished. This lesson may be true for their relationship with their parents, but the same reasoning does not apply to God's relationship with us. God does not *react* to us, God *acts*. His love for us does not come because of what we have done. His love exists first, before we do anything at all. He loves us only because we *are*. We are God's children and he made us because he loves us. Unless we as parents understand this concept, we cannot expect our children to learn of God's unlimited and unconditional love.

The Prodigal Son story (Lk 15:11–32) shows us the wayward son who came home intending to bargain with the father. "If I come home and tell him how sorry I am, then he will at least give me enough to eat." The young man never got any words out of his mouth. His father loved and forgave him even before his apology. The father's love was unconditional. Bargaining was unnecessary.

107

In helping our children through the grieving process, it is well to remember this parable and show by our actions that true love forgives no matter what they do.

Depression

In Chapter 4, I mentioned that depression was anger turned in on oneself. It is true for children. They will internalize their emotions, finding them almost impossible to verbalize. Feelings of guilt and fear will predominate. Some of the thoughts that run through their heads might run like this:

"Dad was angry at me the day before he died. If I hadn't been so bad then he wouldn't have had that heart attack. I caused his death."

"If I had been a better son (daughter), Mom wouldn't have gotten so sick and would still be here with me."

"I should have helped Dad more around the house. Then he wouldn't have died."

"Maybe my fight with my brother (sister) brought on Mom's death."

Again, the ifs, shoulds and oughts pile up guilt until the children can no longer carry the load. Depression sets in.

Talking about realistic and unrealistic guilt is important for children, just as it is for adults. Explaining the disease or accident in understandable terms and helping them see that no one had control over Dad's death are good ways to counteract depression. Assuring them that those feelings are normal for all people, not just children, is another way to reassure them and bring a measure of peace into their lives.

108

In watching for signs of depression in their children, parents need to be aware that each age group will have its own signals. Pre-schoolers may regress to earlier forms of behavior, temporarily losing the recently gained control of bladder and bowels. They may experience a loss of appetite and be unable to eat properly. For school-age children and pre-teenagers, the first indication may be a drop in grades. Nightmares and sleep-walking may become a problem. There may be difficulty with friendships or young people may withdraw from their peer group because they are feeling different from those who come from "real families," not single-parent homes.

One guidance counselor says that the most important thing a parent can do is to help the child to bring his or her feelings to the surface. Those emotions which are churning around inside a child can cause behavior problems at home and at school. Most importantly it puts up a big road block which prevents the child from moving toward acceptance and healing.

If you fail in repeated attempts to get a child to look at those feelings, then certainly a session or two of professional counseling is called for. A neutral party, one outside the family, can bring the suppressed emotions to the surface and assure the child that it is O.K. to have those feelings. Often children do not want to verbalize their feelings because it might hurt their grieving mother or father. Art and play therapy is an especially effective way to allow the child to express anxieties that otherwise would not appear. A professional counselor is trained to interpret the child's reactions and help deal with feelings.

God does not take away parents because the children were bad, because they had a fight with a brother or sister, or because they had bad thoughts. There are many reasons why people die. Dealing with the mystery of death is part of growing up. As modern, rush-to-get-it-done people we don't often reflect that all life is a preparation for death. Maybe it would help us to read *When Bad Things Happen to Good People*, where author Rabbi Kushner suggests that the question is not "Why?" but "What can I learn from this event in my life?"

Children and Illness

"I don't feel good. Do I have to go to school?"

"My tummy hurts."

"My ear hurts. I think I had better stay home today."

"I don't want to play with my friend Susie."

On the social readjustment rating scale developed by Thomas H. Holmes and Richard Rahe, the death of a close family member rates number five on the list of stressors that bring on life crises (*Journal of Psychosomatic Research*). Recent medical studies show that 80 to 90 percent of all illness is stress-related. We should not be surprised then when our children develop illness or disease right after a parent's death.

Within three months of Jim's death, my youngest daughter Jenny was in the hospital with pneumonia. Chronic asthma attacks sent her back every fall for the next three years. Even at the age of two, her body knew that something was wrong.

For many years Steve was plagued with ear infections that were extremely painful. He also had a

hard time going to school, and it took all my inge-
nuity to get him to leave home in the morning.

Lyn Caine's book, *Widow*, taught me that even
very young children grieve and need to talk out their
feelings. Neither Steve nor Jenny had any conscious
memories of their father, since he died when they
were two and three years old. At bedtime I started
telling them stories about their dad. We talked about
some of the things Jim had done with them when
they were babies, the pet names he had for them and
how very much he loved them. We talked about his
diabetes, the many times he had been hospitalized
and how sick he had been. That proved to be the
opening Steve needed, for he confided his deep concern that I might disappear some day while he was at
school and then, "Who would take care of me?" Although my oldest daughter had agreed to be guard-
ian for the two minor children in the event of my
death, I had not thought to tell them! When Steve
heard that Peggy would be in charge, you could see
the relief on his face.

Not only was this a time of emotional healing for
our family, but Steve's earaches virtually disappeared. There was no more trouble getting him to
school in the morning.

It is not easy to distinguish between physical illness and depression in children. If one infection or
upset after another appears, then it is time to look at
the whole picture and say, "Could this be unresolved
feelings that we haven't talked about?" There have
been many studies that confirmed what I learned
from Steve: Our feelings, fears, anxieties and emotions have a definite effect on the wellness or illness
of our bodies.

Acceptance

God grant me the serenity to accept
  the things I cannot change,
the courage to change the things I can
and the wisdom to know the difference.
                            — Alcoholics Anonymous

Slowly I learned that answering my children's questions and allaying their fears was an effective way for them and me to move toward acceptance. In searching for the right words to reassure them, I automatically found solutions for some of my seemingly insurmountable problems. This proved to be a circle of healing. When I dealt with my own grief the children responded the same way. Their hurts lessened. By taking care of myself I helped my children and they helped me.

Growing up is hard work whether in a one-parent or two-parent home. Anxiety, vulnerability and insecurity are very close to the surface during the teen years. Sometimes youthful impulses can be very frightening. Young people need to know that no matter what happens or what they do, they are still loved. They need someone who can set reasonable limits on their own developing and sometimes out-of-hand outbursts.

We do need to be aware of one mistake that frequently surfaces because of our pain and hurt. During their teen years, young people need parents as parents, not as friends. It is very easy for a single parent to look on an adolescent, teenager or even an adult child as someone to lean on when the going gets difficult. We must remember that we are still their parents. They are not our peers and we do them a grave injustice if we look to them for our emotional support. We have an obligation to find other people who we can confide in, other groups who will listen to us when the grief is overwhelming.

Never underestimate your children's ability to sense when something is wrong. They are tuned into every mood and emotion that we have. That is why even very young children know when a parent finds a measure of peace and acceptance. If our children's intuition tells them we have found some meaning in our lives and have not just resigned ourselves to the death of our loved one, they will follow our lead. Their path may be lined with the same stones and hidden traps that we found. They may stumble and fall just as we did. Our role is to be there with them when they need support, understanding and love.

A favorite prayer for my single-parent family is a paraphrase from one in *The Pope's Family Prayer Book*:

> Lord, help my children to know the road you
>   have chosen for them:
> may they give you glory and attain salvation.
> Sustain them with your strength,
>   and let them not be satisfied with easy
>   goals.
> Enlighten me, their mother (father)
>   that I may help them to recognize their
>   calling in life
>   and respond to it generously.
> May I put no obstacle in the way of your inner
>   guidance.

Nine

Closing the Door Gently

Some day we may be able to look back and realize that a death in the family was a turning point in our lives. Will we delay, fight or facilitate this change of direction? Probably all three. Change, the process of becoming different, frightens us. We are always afraid of the unknown, unwilling to step off into the darkness of the future. The old way is easier even if it causes pain. How do we find the courage to change?

One of the most difficult human experiences is letting go, and we are asked to do that in some manner or another very often. What do I mean by "letting go"? It is *not* forgetting my loved one, burying memories, or resigning myself to the status quo. It is facing the past honestly and squarely, forgiving myself for all I have contributed to past hurts. It is releasing anger, bitterness and hatred — those negative feelings and emotions that tangle up life so I can't move forward. Letting go is allowing myself to see the positive in the past, truly accepting the present and looking forward to the future.

From birth to death, life is a process of letting go, a series of little dyings that take us to our resurrection. In releasing those things that prevent us from growing emotionally, spiritually and physically, we are able to look ahead, trust and hope again. We know that God will guide us in the right direction and we will find the joy of new life and growth.

St. Paul assures us: "We are afflicted, but not crushed; perplexed, but not driven to despair" (2 Cor 4:8–9, Lectionary version).

When I was trying to decide if I should continue my education, I had to let go of my old role as mother and homemaker, leave the relative security of my home (die to that way of life) and trust that God was calling me to a new path. In letting go, I experienced death, but the decision brought me to a new joy in life — resurrection. I was following Jesus, God's son, who also had to die before he could rise again.

One image that helped me move on is that of closing the door on my past. In doing this I looked at the positive and negative aspects of my life, not denying, regretting, or clinging to those memories, but remembering with love. Several years after Jim died I found a way to close that door gently but firmly. I wrote him a letter.

Dear Jim,

It has been many, many years since my last letter to you. I hardly know how to start. I have so many memories of the 22 years we were together that I hardly know where to begin. Those have been growth-filled, upsetting, loving, hurting, exciting and overwhelming years — definitely not dull or boring.

Those first few years, as we learned to know and love each other, were filled with anxiety also. I miscarried three times and we thought there would never be any children. We even talked about adoption. How wrong we were! God had other plans for us. We finally got our beautiful baby girl, Peggy, and then when Dan was born you couldn't believe the doctor's good news. You had read somewhere that most miscarriages were boys, so you were very sure that all the boys had been lost. How thrilled both of us were with that red-haired Curry boy.

The babies came fast and furious those first years, seven children in nine years. They took all my time and energy and I know I had little time left for our relationship when they were little. Forgive me. Hindsight is a good teacher. There is one thing in my life that I would do differently if I had another chance. I would give top priority to you and the communication that is so necessary for a good, loving relationship. The children would be second in line.

I was a scared, insecure little girl of 43. You waited so long for me to grow up, and I really didn't do much of that until after you died. I was so bound up in what people would think, so afraid of being different from everybody else, so sure that to be loved I had to be perfect. "If I show you who I really am, you

117

won't love me." There were so many walls and barriers between us. Nevertheless, we had a good marriage. You were a good man, thoughtful and loving to me, even if you didn't understand the feminine psyche too well. You had grown up with two brothers and no sisters. But then I must have been a trial to you also, for I had grown up with two sisters and no brothers. All those noisy, wrestling males in our family were pretty foreign to me. But we grew and adapted and loved them all.

Today our five boys and four girls are our pride and joy, and I wouldn't change a minute of our life together. I must admit, however, that joy in all nine children is one I grew into. I cried many buckets of tears with the last two pregnancies. How could I be pregnant again when your health was steadily declining? What would I do with all those children if you died? Trust in God is a long time coming.

Many of these intervening years have been spent looking into me and realizing that I created those walls, and oh! the guilt that I heaped upon myself. I am so sorry for all we did not have: for the lack of communication and the inability to show each other who we really were, the lack of trust. Yet today I realize at that time in our lives we knew no better. I can't blame myself for not giving things that I didn't have to give. The past is gone. The present is now. And it is in this present that I can do something about the future.

I am at an important milestone in my life: a closing of the door on our marriage. It has taken many years for me to grow to this point. I have moved back and forth through all the stages of grief. This period of my life is over, with all the sadness and painfulness that goes with partings. Now a new beginning is here, just like the sunrise that I saw this February morning. I am ready to go on and see what the Lord has waiting for me. I know it will not be more than I can handle. God will give me all the help I need.

I love you Jim. I always will. I may marry again some day if that is what God has planned. As for now, I feel able to handle what is ahead of me. I can never forget what we had, but now, on to a new beginning.

Love,
Cathy

Earlier I had taken my wedding and engagement rings off and put them on at least a dozen times. If I wasn't married anymore who was I? Mrs. James Curry or Cathleen Curry? Two days after I wrote this letter, the rings came off to stay. I had written a letter of closure and knew I was single again. I had let go.

Once I closed the door on my past, I didn't have to open it again, although I can, for it is not locked. My door has a glass window so I can look back and remember without letting all those negative emotions overwhelm me.

By now you must realize that time alone does not heal grief. Donald R. Bourcier, C.F.A., says that "the best memorial to a loved one is a full growing life" (*Death Education*). Using grief as a building block for your own personal growth is the only way to leave the depths of depression.

As I wrote in my letter, I was at a new milestone in my life. You too have decisions to make, new directions to turn. Workshops and seminars on parenting, stress reduction, self-esteem, financial affairs and spirituality can point the way, but there are still difficult steps to take. Moving away from the familiar is the only way to put ourselves on the road to recovery.

Reaching out to someone else who is hurting pulls me out of the doldrums. Volunteer work at hospitals, soup kitchens, battered women's residences, support groups, visiting the sick and elderly, going back to school, going for career counseling, finding a spiritual director — the list is endless. You are the only one who can decide which step to take first. Never forget that God is ready and willing to help when you ask. Fifteen minutes of solitude and silence each morning can help you with your decision.

Memories help the whole family heal, especially the humorous ones. One of our favorite stories is about Jim taking five-year-old Tim for a one-day truck trip. His interminable questions wore Daddy out. "What's that, Daddy?" "Why does that happen, Daddy?" "When are we going to get there, Daddy?" Finally Jim said, "Tim, why don't you count the telephone poles?" (That wouldn't work now. All the telephone lines are underground.) Now Tim, whose son is going through the same stage, is learning how to cope with endless questions.

Memories can enrich your life for many years. How about starting your Christmas festivities with a special story or memory from each member of the family? Give a little advance notice and you might be surprised at some of the tales that appear. Are there enough funds to set up a memorial or a scholarship in memory of your loved one? How about writing a story that could be dedicated to him or her? Many husbands or wives take over the family business, keeping involved in their spouse's interests.

120

All these memories can be turned into peace and joy. God has promised that many times in his scriptures.

> In the tender compassion of our God
> the dawn from on high shall break upon us,
> to shine on those who dwell in darkness
> and the shadow of death
> and to guide our feet into the way of peace
> (Lk 1:78–79).

> I shall change their mourning into gladness,
> comfort them, give them joy after their troubles
> (Jer 31:13).

The meaning of human suffering is a mystery. We can never fully penetrate to the center of this mystery. We can, however, use our suffering to deepen our understanding of life, and in that way draw closer to God.

I have tried to avoid preaching, for I firmly believe that each one of us is different, has unique life experiences and relates to those experiences in different ways. By sharing with you how I related to sadness and grief, I hope I have helped you to choose to deal creatively with yours.

The choice is up to you. Staying away from risks, avoiding change in life is safe. The question is, "Will you be safe and stagnate, or will you risk and find your reward?" The risk is not as great as you think. God is with you every step of the way.

Your life is a beautiful jewel with many facets of joy, sadness, despair, love, sorrow and peace. Each cut of the jewel shows a different aspect reflecting God's glory. If you take this precious stone and hide it in a drawer, it will grow dull and lifeless. But if you

121

mount it in a beautiful setting, your life will shine and sparkle as it never has before.

> Come, take heart,
> Find healing.
> Live again —
> Love again —
> Maybe even more than you did before.

J. J. Young, C.S.P.

Reading List

(Some of these books may be out of print. Very likely they can be found in libraries.)

SPIRITUALITY

Clinging, Emilie Griffin, Harper & Row, San Francisco, 1984.

Contemplative Prayer, Thomas Merton, Image Book, Doubleday & Co., Garden City, NY, 1971.

Daily We Touch Him, M. Basil Pennington, O.C.S.O., Image Book, Doubleday & Co., 1979.

He Touched Me, John Powell, SJ, Argus Communications, Niles, IL, 1974.

Lord Hear Our Prayer, Thomas McNally, C.S.C. and William G. Storey, D.M.S., Ave Maria Press, Notre Dame, IN, 1978.

Morning and Evening Prayer: Selections from the Liturgy of the Hours , Edited by Rev. D. Joseph Finnerty, Rev. George J. Ryan, Regina Press, NY, 1978.

Opening to God, Thomas H. Green, S.J., Ave Maria Press, Notre Dame, IN 1977.

Prayer of the Heart, George A. Maloney, S.J., Ave Maria Press, Notre Dame, IN, 1981.

Prayer Talk, William V. Coleman, Ave Maria Press, Notre Dame, IN, 1983.

The Daily Study Bible Series, Revised Edition, William Barclay, Westminster Press, Philadelphia, 1975.

The Imitation of Christ, Thomas à Kempis: A Timeless Classic for Contemporary Readers, William C. Creasy, Ave Maria Press, Notre Dame, IN, 1989.

The Way of the Pilgrim, translated by R.M. French, Ballantine Books, New York, 1974.

Walking With Loneliness, Paula Ripple, F.S.P.A., Ave Maria Press, Notre Dame, IN, 1982.

With Open Hands, Henri J.M. Nouwen, Ave Maria Press, Notre Dame, IN, 1972.

GRIEF

A Grief Observed, C.S. Lewis, Seabury Press, New York, 1961.

But I Never Thought He'd Die, Miriam Baker Nye, Westminster Press, Philadelphia, 1978.

Death, the Final Stage of Growth, Elisabeth Kubler-Ross, Prentice-Hall Inc., Englewood Cliffs, NJ, 1975.

Good Grief, Granger E. Westberg, Fortress Press, Philadelphia, 1971.

How to Survive the Loss of a Love, Colgrove, Bloomfield & McWilliams, Bantam, New York, 1976.

Loneliness, Clark E. Moustakas, Spectrum/Prentice-Hall, Inc., 1961.

On Death and Dying, Elisabeth Kubler-Ross, Macmillan Publishing Co., New York, 1969.

The Art of Loving, Erich Fromm, Bantam Books, New York, 1956.

The Courage to Grieve, Judy Tatelbaum, Harper & Row, New York, 1980.

The Wounded Healer, Henri J.M. Nouwen, Image/Doubleday, Garden City, NY, 1979.

Time Out for Grief, Jean Gannon Jones, Our Sunday Visitor, Inc., Huntington, IN, 1979.

When Bad Things Happen to Good People, Harold S. Kushner, Avon Books Inc., New York, 1981.

Widow, Lynn Caine, William Morrow & Co., Inc., New York, 1974.

Working It Through, Elisabeth Kubler-Ross, Macmillan Publishing Co., New York, 1982.

PSYCHOLOGY

Free to Be Human, Eugene Kennedy, Cornerstone Library/Simon & Schuster, New York, 1979.

Fully Human, Fully Alive, John J. Powell, S.J., Argus Communications, Niles, IL, 1976.

Mirror, Mirror on the Wall: The Art of Talking with Yourself, John Powers, Twenty-Third Publications, Mystic, CT, 1987.

The Joy of Being Human, Eugene Kennedy, Image/Doubleday, Garden City, NY, 1974.

Why Am I Afraid to Tell You Who I Am?, John Powell, S.J., Argus Communications, Niles, IL, 1969.

MAGAZINES

Praying, 115 E. Armour Blvd., Kansas City, MO 64111.

St. Anthony Messenger, 1615 Republic St., Cincinnati, OH 45210.

U.S. Catholic, 205 W. Monroe St., Chicago, IL 60606.

MISCELLANEOUS REFERENCES

Beginning Experience Central Office, 305 Michigan Ave., Detroit, MI 48226.

What Color Is My Parachute? Richard Nelson Bolles, Ten Speed Press, Berkeley, CA, 1989. (A new edition of this career planning book is printed each year.)

For a list of Certified Financial Planners write:
College for Financial Planning
9725 E. Hampden Ave.
Denver, CO 80231–4993
(303) 755–7101

Cooperative Extension Service
(Check telephone book under Government Offi
Extension Services, local county.)

Displaced Homemakers Network
1411 K St. N.W.
Washington, DC 20005
(202) 628–6767